21 世纪高职高专机电系列技能型规划教材

模具专业英语图解教程

主　编　李东君
副主编　钱晓琳　唐　妍

北京大学出版社
PEKING UNIVERSITY PRESS

内容简介

本书的内容均选自英、美国家专业教材及专业刊物中的原文，共 7 个项目，28 个工作任务，内容涉及机械基础(材料及热处理、制图、常用零件和传统加工)、冷冲压工艺及模具、塑料模具、模具成型机械、模具制造技术(数控加工和特种加工)、模具常用术语、CAD/CAM、模具寿命和失效，涵盖了模具设计与制造专业所需的技术知识。

本书实务性强，由项目引领，任务驱动，适合作为高职高专院校模具相关专业的英语教材，也可作为模具企业培训教材，还适合作为模具管理人员的自学参考书。

图书在版编目(CIP)数据

模具专业英语图解教程/李东君主编. —北京：北京大学出版社，2013.7
(21 世纪高职高专机电系列技能型规划教材)
ISBN 978-7-301-22678-0

Ⅰ.①模… Ⅱ.①李… Ⅲ.①模具—英语—高等职业教育—教材 Ⅳ.①H31

中国版本图书馆 CIP 数据核字(2013)第 136845 号

书　　　名：	模具专业英语图解教程
著作责任者：	李东君　主编
策 划 编 辑：	张永见
责 任 编 辑：	李娉婷
标 准 书 号：	ISBN 978-7-301-22678-0/TH・0354
出 版 发 行：	北京大学出版社
地　　　址：	北京市海淀区成府路 205 号　邮编：100871
网　　　址：	http://www.pup.cn　新浪官方微博：@北京大学出版社
电 子 信 箱：	pup_6@163.com
电　　　话：	邮购部 62752015　发行部 62750672　编辑部 62750667　出版部 62754962
印　刷　者：	北京虎彩文化传播有限公司
经　销　者：	新华书店
	787 毫米×1092 毫米　16 开本　10.5 印张　236 千字
	2013 年 7 月第 1 版　2022 年 8 月第 4 次印刷
定　　　价：	32.00 元

未经许可，不得以任何方式复制或抄袭本书之部分或全部内容。
版权所有，侵权必究
举报电话：010-62752024　电子信箱：fd@pup.pku.edu.cn

前 言

在快速发展的模具设计与制造领域，人们需要使用大量的原版英语技术资料和掌握国外最新的技术信息与动态，因此，拥有良好的英语水平对于专业技术的学习和提高有着举足轻重的作用。

本书根据教育部"关于加强高职高专教育教材建设的若干意见"和国家关于高职高专教材新编专业教材的最新指导思想而编写，以项目引领、任务驱动，本书编写大纲已在多所高职院校执行。

本书以提高学生专业英语阅读能力，扩展和深化学生对模具设计和制造领域关键技术的认知，为学生的职业生涯可持续发展搭建平台为目的，本着先进、实用、简明、系统的组织原则，从以高职教育实践为主的实际出发，结合作者多年的专业英语教学实践编写而成。

本书在编写过程中力求体现下列特点。

(1) 面向广大高职教育对象，重点在于扩充学生的专业英语词汇量，提高读者的科技英语阅读能力。

(2) 以培养模具设计与制造专业能力为目标选取文章，以项目模块式结构进行组织，便于教师灵活选用。

(3) 在内容上注重选材的实用，在形式上注重图文并茂，且在正文的右侧配有生词注释，疑难句有注释，便于读者阅读。

(4) 文章均为原版英语文献，英语表达地道，力求兼顾知识的基础性与专业性，同时反映专业发展的新趋势。

本书由南京交通职业技术学院李东君担任主编，钱晓琳、唐妍担任副主编。李东君负责全书的统稿。由于编者水平和经验有限，书中仍可能存在一些疏漏，恳请教师和读者批评指正，以便修订时改进。

编 者

2013 年 2 月

目 录

Project 1 Foundations of Mechanics ... 1

- Task 1.1 Engineering Drawing ... 1
- Task 1.2 Materials' Categories and Properties ... 5
- Task 1.3 Steels ... 8
- Task 1.4 Cast Iron ... 12
- Task 1.5 Polymers ... 14
- Task 1.6 Heat Treatment of Steel ... 18
- Task 1.7 Die Materials ... 23

Project 2 Forming Machines ... 25

- Task 2.1 Presses ... 25
- Task 2.2 Injection-molding Machines ... 31

Project 3 Press Forming Processes and Dies ... 36

- Task 3.1 Forging ... 36
- Task 3.2 Blanking Principles ... 39
- Task 3.3 Piercing and Blanking Die ... 43
- Task 3.4 Bending Die ... 47

Project 4 Plastic Forming Processes and Molds ... 51

- Task 4.1 Injection Mold ... 51
- Task 4.2 Compression Mold ... 53
- Task 4.3 Major Parts Used for an Ejection System ... 54

Project 5 The Computers' Applications in Industry ... 58

- Task 5.1 CAD/CAM ... 58
- Task 5.2 CAD/CAM's Applications ... 61

Project 6 Manufacturing Technology of Die/Mold ... 66

- Task 6.1 The Applications of NC/CNC ... 66
- Task 6.2 NC Operation Control Panel ... 69
- Task 6.3 NC/CNC Machines' Screen Display Reading ... 74
- Task 6.4 NC Programming ... 77

  Task 6.5 Safety Notes for CNC Machine Operations 83
  Task 6.6 Fault Diagnosis and Action 86
  Task 6.7 Types of Control Devices 88
  Task 6.8 Non-traditional Manufacturing Processes 92

Project 7 Life and Failure of Die 102
  Task 7.1 Life and Failure of Die 102
  Task 7.2 Effects of Surface Treatment and Lubricant on Die Life 105

Reading Materials 108

参考译文 120

References 157

Project 1

Foundations of Mechanics

Task 1.1 Engineering Drawing

Engineering drawing is an abstract universal language used to represent a designer's idea to others and the most accepted medium of communication in all aspects of industrial and engineering work.[1]

abstract 抽象的
universal 通用的
represent 表达
aspect 方面
manufacture 制造
multiview 多视图

In today's modern manufacturing industry, the standard type of drawings is the multiview drawing (Fig.1.1). A multiview drawing usually contains two or three views (front, top, and side). Each view is an orthographic projection of a plane. In the United States and Canada, the third-angle projection is used (Fig.1.2).

orthographic 正交
projection 投影

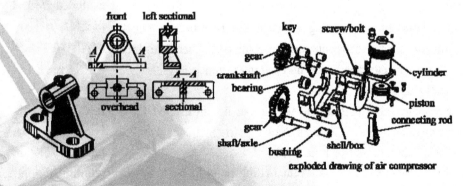

Fig. 1.1 Types of views

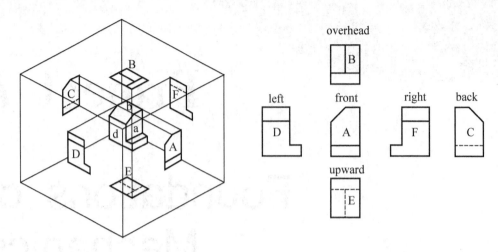

Fig. 1.2   Third-angle projection

1. Coordinate System

The basic of all input AutoCAD is the Cartesian coordinate system, and the various methods of input (absolute or relative) rely on this system. In addition, AutoCAD has two internal coordinate systems to help you keep track of where you are in a drawing: the World Coordinate System (WCS) and the User Coordinate System (UCS). The fixed Cartesian coordinate system locates all points on an AutoCAD drawing by defining a series of positive and negative axes to locate positions in space.[2]

2. Types of Views

There are many view types used in engineering drawing: projection, auxiliary, general, detailed, revolved, half, sectional, exploded, partial, etc.[3]

3. Fits

The fit between two mating parts is the relationship which results from the clearance or interference obtained.[4] There are three classes of fit, namely, clearance, transition and interference.

4. Interchangeability

An interchangeable part is one which can be substituted for a similar part manufactured to the same drawing. The interchangeability of parts is based upon these two functions.

① It is necessary for the relevant mating parts to be designed incorporating limits of size.

② The parts must be made within the specified limits.

5. Limits of Size (Dimension Tolerance)

In deciding the limits necessary for a particular dimension, there

coordinate 坐标
Cartesian 笛卡尔
absolute 绝对的
relative 相对的
internal 内部的
track 痕迹，踪迹
locate 定位
define 定义
positive 正的
negative 负的

auxiliary 辅助的
revolve 旋转
exploded 爆破的
fit 配合
interference 过盈，干涉
transition 过渡
interchange 互换
substitute 替代

function 功能，作用
relevant 相关的
mating 配合，装配
incorporating 一体的
dimension 尺寸
tolerance 公差

are 3 considerations: functional importance, interchangeability and economics. To assist the designer to choose limits and fits and to encourage uniformity throughout the world industry, a number of limit-and-fit systems have been published.

consideration 考虑事项

uniformity 统一，一致

Notes

1. Engineering drawing is an abstract universal language used to represent a designer's idea to others and the most accepted medium of communication in all aspects of industrial and engineering work.

工程制图是向别人表达设计师意图的一种抽象的通用语言，它是在工业和工程中的各个方面使用最普遍的沟通媒介。

2. The fixed Cartesian coordinate system locates all points on an AutoCAD drawing by defining a series of positive and negative axes to locate positions in space.

固定的笛卡儿坐标系是通过定义一系列用以确定空间位置的正负轴来定位 AutoCAD 图中的所有点的。

动词不定式短语 to locate positions in space 是 a series of positive and negative axes 的后置定语，说明 axes 的作用。

by defining … in space 是整句的方式状语，说明定位点的方法。

3. There are many view types used in engineering drawing: projection, auxiliary, general, detailed, revolved, half, sectional, explosive, partial, etc.

工程制图有许多视图类型：投影视图、辅助视图、全视图、细节放大视图、旋转视图、半视图、剖视图、爆炸视图、局部视图等。

4. The fit between two mating parts is the relationship which results from the clearance or interference obtained.

两个装配零件间的配合是一种由装配时所产生的间隙或过盈而引发的关系。

此句中 which results … obtained 是 the relationship 的定语从句。

 New Words and Expressions

abstract [ˈæbstrækt] adj. 抽象的，深奥的
universal [ˌjuːniˈvəːsəl] adj. 普遍的，通用的
represent [ˌriːpriˈzent] vt. 表现，描绘，表达
aspect [ˈæspekt] n. 方面，样子
manufacture [ˌmænjuˈfæktʃə] v. & n. 制造
multiview [mʌltivjuː] n. 多视图
orthographic [ˌɔːθəˈɡræfik] adj. 正交的
projection [prəˈdʒekʃən] n. 投影(法)

negative [ˈneɡətiv] adj. 负的，否定的
auxiliary [ɔːɡˈziljəri] adj. 辅助的，补助的
revolve [riˈvɔlv] v. (使)旋转，循环出现
exploded [iksˈpləudid] adj. 爆破的，打破的
fit [fit] v. & n. 配合，装配，适合
interference [ˌintəˈfiərəns] n. 过盈，干涉
transition [trænˈziʒən] n. 过渡，变迁
interchange [ˌintəˈtʃeindʒ] v. 互换
substitute [ˈsʌbstitjuːt] v. 替代 n. 替代品

coordinate [kəuˈɔːdinit] n. 坐标
Cartesian [kɑːˈtiːzjən] adj. 笛卡儿的
absolute [ˈæbsəluːt] adj. 绝对的
relative [ˈrelətiv] adj. 相对的，有关系的
internal [inˈtəːnl] adj. 内部的
track [træk] n. 痕迹，踪迹
locate [ləuˈkeit] v. 定位，位于，查找……地点
define [diˈfain] vt. 定义，详细说明
positive [ˈpɔzətiv] adj. 正的，积极的，绝对的

function [ˈfʌŋkʃən] n. 功能，作用，职责
relevant [ˈrelivənt] adj. 相关的
mating [ˈmeitiŋ] n. 配合，装配 adj. 啮合的
incorporating [inˈkɔːpəreit] adj. 一体的
　　　　　　　v. 合并
dimension [diˈmenʃən] n. 尺寸，维度，元
tolerance [ˈtɔlərəns] n. 公差 v. 规定公差
consideration [kənsidəˈreiʃən] n. 考虑事项
uniformity [juːniˈfɔːmiti] n. 统一，一致，均匀

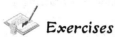

Exercises

I. Complete the following sentences according to the text.

1. Coordinate values are divided into two types that are _____ and _____in Cartesian coordinate system.

2. In AutoCAD, there are two internal coordinate systems _____ and _____to help you keep your track of where you are in a drawing.

3. An orthographic projection of an object can be seen from the _____, top, and right side, etc..

4. Engineering drawing is an _____, which is used to represent a designer's idea to others.

5. _____ projection is used in America and Canada.

II. Translate the following phrases into Chinese or English.

1. 投　影_____　　2. 视　图_____　　3. 配　合_____
4. 公　差_____　　5. 互换性_____　　6. 剖视图_____
7. clearance, transition and interference _____
8. third-angle projection _____

III. Answer the following questions according to the text.

1. How many types of views are there in our text ? Please give their names.

2. What are the two functions the interchangeability of parts is based on ?

Task 1.2 Materials' Categories and Properties

The principal engineering materials can be divided into three major categories: ferrous materials, nonferrous materials and nonmetallic materials. Ferrous materials have iron as a base metal and include tool steel, alloy steel, carbon steel and cast iron. Nonferrous materials have a base metal other than iron and include aluminum, magnesium, zinc, lead, bismuth, copper and a variety of alloys. Nonmetallic materials are those materials such as woods, plastic, rubbers, epoxy resins, ceramics and diamonds that do not have a metallic base.

To properly select a material, there are several physical and mechanical properties you should understand to determine how the material you select will affect the function and operation.[1]

Physical and mechanical properties are those characteristics of a material which control how the material will react under certain condition. Physical properties are those properties which are natural in the material and cannot be permanently altered without changing the material itself. These properties include weight, color, thermal and electrical conductivity, rate of thermal expansion and melting point. The mechanical properties of a material are those properties which can be permanently altered by thermal or mechanical treatment. These properties include strength, hardness, ductility, wear resistance, toughness, brittleness, plasticity, malleability and modulus of elasticity.

In most applications, more than one type of material will be satisfactory and a final choice will normally be governed by material availability and economic considerations.

Depending on the processing parameters for the various processing methods, the length of the production run and the number of finished parts to be produced, molds must satisfy a great variety of requirement. It is therefore

---

ferrous 含铁的

alloy 合金

magnesium 镁
lead 铅
bismuth 铋
epoxy resin 环氧树脂
ceramics 陶瓷

mechanical 机械的
function 功能，运行

permanently 永久地
alter 改变
thermal conductivity 导热性
expansion 膨胀

ductility 韧性，延展性
malleability 可锻性
modulus of elasticity 弹性模量

availability 可利用性
consideration 事项
price-to-performance ratio 性价比
processing parameter 工艺参数

not surprising that, molds can be made from a very broad spectrum of materials, including such exotic materials as paper match and plaster.[2] However, because most processes require high pressures, and often combined with high temperature, metals still represent by far the most important material group, with steel being the predominant metal. It is interesting in this regard that, in many cases, the selection of the mold material is not only a question of material properties and an optimum price-to-performance ratio but also that the methods used to produce the mold, and thus the entire design can be influenced.[3]

spectrum 系列，谱型
exotic 奇异的

predominant 主导的

optimum 最适宜的

Notes

1. To properly select a material, there are several physical and mechanical properties you should understand to determine how the material you select will affect the function and operation.

为了恰当地选择材料，必须掌握材料的一些物理性能和机械性能，以便确定所选的材料对功能和操作有何影响。

此句主干为 there be 句型，you should understand 和 you select 均为定语从句，to properly select a material 为目的状语，to determine how the material…为结果状语。

2. It is therefore not surprising that, molds can be made from a very broad spectrum of materials, including such exotic materials as paper match and plaster.

因此，模具可由多种材料制成，包括像纸张、石膏这样的奇异材料，也就不奇怪了。

此句为强调句型，强调表语 not surprising。

3. It is interesting in this regard that, in many cases, the selection of the mold material is not only a question of material properties and an optimum price-to-performance ratio but also that the methods used to produce the mold, and thus the entire design can be influenced.

有趣的是，在许多情况下，选择模具材料不仅要考虑材料的性能和最佳的性价比，还要考虑模具的制造方法，因而整体设计会受到这些因素的影响。

此句为强调句型，强调表语 interesting。

New words and Expressions

category [ˈkætigəri] n. 种类，[逻]范畴
property [ˈprɔpəti] n. 财产，性质，特性
ferrous [ˈferəs] adj. 铁的，含铁的
alloy [ˈælɔi] n. 合金

strength [streŋθ] n. 强度；力，力量
hardness [ˈhɑːdnis] n. 硬，硬度
ductility [dʌkˈtiliti] n. 塑性，韧性，柔软
wear resistance 耐磨性

Project 1 Foundations of Mechanics

carbon steel 碳钢
cast iron 铸铁
aluminum [əˈljuːminəm] n. 铝(Al)
magnesium [mægˈniːzjəm] n. 镁(Mg)
zinc [ziŋk] n. 锌(Zn)
lead [liːd] n. 铅(Pb)
bismuth [ˈbizməθ] n. 铋(Bi)
copper [ˈkɔpə] n. 铜(Cu)
rubber [ˈrʌbə] n. 橡胶,橡皮
epoxy [eˈpɔksi] adj. 环氧的
resin [ˈrezin] n. 树脂
ceramics [siˈræmiks] n. 陶器；陶瓷制品
mechanical [miˈkænikl] adj. 机械的,机械制的
function [ˈfʌŋkʃən] n. 功能,活动,运行
operation [ˌɔpəˈreiʃən] n. 运转,操作,手术
characteristic [ˌkæriktəˈristik] n. 特性,特征
permanently [ˈpəːmənəntli] adv. 永久地,不变地
alter [ˈɔːltə] v. 改变
thermal [ˈθəːməl] adj. 热的,热量的
conductivity [ˌkɔndʌkˈtiviti] n. 传导性
expansion [iksˈpænʃən] n. 扩充,膨胀
melting point 熔点
treatment [ˈtriːtmənt] n. 处理,对待,治疗

toughness [ˈtʌfnis] n. 刚性,韧性
brittleness [ˈbritlnis] n. 脆性,脆度；脆弱性
plasticity [plæsˈtisiti] n. 塑性,可塑性
malleability [ˌmæliəˈbiliti] n. (金属的)可锻性
modulus [ˈmɔdjuləs] n. 模数,系数
elasticity [ilæsˈtisiti] n. 弹性,弹力
application [ˌæpliˈkeiʃən] n. 应用,运用
satisfactory [sætisˈfæktəri] adj. 令人满意的
govern [ˈgʌv(ə)n] v. 控制,指导,决定
availability [əˌveiləˈbiliti] n. 可利用性
economic [ˌiːkəˈnɔmik] adj. 经济的
consideration [kənsidəˈreiʃən] n. 事项,考虑
processing [prəuˈsesiŋ] n. 加工,工艺过程
parameter [pəˈræmitə] n. 参数,参量
run [rʌn] n. 运行,管理
spectrum [ˈspektrəm] n. 型谱,光谱,频谱
exotic [igˈzɔtik] adj. 奇异的,异国情调的
plaster [ˈplɑːstə] n. 石膏,灰泥,膏药
combine [kəmˈbain] v. (使)联合,(使)结合
predominant [priˈdɔminənt] adj. 主导的
optimum [ˈɔptiməm] n.& adj. 最适宜(的)
price-to-performance ratio 性价比
influence [ˈinfluəns] vt. 影响,改变
in this regard 关于此事,在这点上
by far (修饰比较级,最高级)……得多；尤其

Exercises

I. Complete the following sentences according to the text.

1. _____ materials, _____ materials and _____ materials are the three major categories of engineering materials.

2. Physical and _____ properties are those characteristics of a material which control how the material will _____ under certain condition.

3. Ferrous materials have _____ as a base metal and include tool steel, _____ steel, _____ steel and _____.

4. The mechanical properties of a material can be permanently altered by _____ or _____.

5. Depending on the _____ for the various processing methods, the length of the production _____ and the number of _____ to be produced, molds must _____ a great variety of requirement.

II. Translate the following phrases into Chinese or English.

1. 强 度_____ 2. 硬 度_____ 3. 刚 度_____
4. 塑 性_____ 5. 弹 性_____ 6. 脆 性_____
7. 导电性_____ 8. 膨胀率_____ 9. 高 温_____
10. an optimum price-to-performance ratio _____
11. processing parameters _____
12. material availability and economic considerations _____

III. Translate the following sentences into Chinese.

1. Nonmetallic materials are those materials such as woods, plastic, rubbers, epoxy resins, ceramics and diamonds that do not have a metallic base.
2. Physical properties are natural in the material and cannot be permanently altered without changing the material itself. These properties include weight, color, thermal and electrical conductivity, rate of thermal expansion and melting point.
3. Because most processes require high pressures, and often combined with high temperature, metals still represent by far the most important material group, with steel being the predominant metal.

Task 1.3   Steels

More than 90% by weight of the metallic materials used by human beings are ferrous alloys. This represents an immense family of engineering materials with a wide range of microstructures and related properties.[1] The majority of engineering designs that require structural load support or power transmission involve ferrous alloys.[2] As a practical matter, these alloys fall into two broad categories based on the carbon in the alloy composition. Steel generally contains between 0.05 and 2.0 wt% carbon. The cast irons generally contain between 2.0 and 4.5 wt% carbon.

immense 极大的
microstructure 微观结构

power 动力，功率
transmission 传递，传送
composition 成分

There are two general kinds of steels: carbon steel and alloy steel.

1. Carbon Steels

Carbon steel contains only iron and carbon, and small amounts of other alloying elements. As the carbon content is increased in carbon steel, the strength, toughness, and hardness are also increased when the metal is heat treated. Carbon steels are the most common and least expensive type of steel used for tools.

(1) Low carbon steel contains from 0.05 to 0.25 wt% carbon. Low carbon steels are soft, tough steels that are easily machined and welded. Due to their low carbon content, these steels cannot be hardened except by case hardening. Low carbon steels are well suited for the following applications: tool bodies, handles, die shoes and similar situations where strength and wear resistance are not required.[3]

machine 机加工
weld 焊接
harden 变硬，淬硬
case hardening 表面淬火
die shoe 模座
wear resistance 耐磨性

(2) Medium carbon steel contains between 0.25 and 0.6 wt% carbon. Medium carbon steels are used where greater strength and toughness is required. Since medium carbon steels have a higher carbon content, they can be heat treated to make parts such as studs, pins, axles, and nuts. Steels in this group are more expensive as well as more difficult to machine and weld than low carbon steels.

stud 柱头螺栓，销子
pin 销，栓
axle 轴
nut 螺母，螺帽

(3) High carbon steel contains between 0.6 and 1.5 wt% carbon. High carbon steels are the most hardenable type of carbon steel and are used frequently for parts where wear resistant is an important factor. Other applications where high carbon steels are well suited include drill bushings, locators, and wear pads. Since the carbon content of these steels is so high, parts made from high carbon steel are normally difficult to machine and weld.

hardenable 可硬化的
frequently 时常，往往

drill bushing 钻套
locator 定位件
wear pad 耐磨垫

2. Alloy Steels

Alloy steel contains some other alloying elements such as chromium, nickel, manganese, vanadium, molybdenum, tungsten, etc. The additional elements make essential improvements in the steels' properties such as higher strength or improved corrosion resistance. However, because the alloying elements invariably increase the materials costs, alloy steels are not normally used for most tools. A composition of 5 wt% total non-carbon additions is an arbitrary boundary between low alloy steels and high alloy steels.

chromium 铬
nickel 镍
tungsten 钨
manganese 锰
vanadium 钒
molybdenum 钼
corrosion resistance 耐腐蚀性
boundary 分界线
moderately 中等的

(1) Low alloy steels are moderately priced due to the absence of large amounts of alloying elements, and they are sufficiently ductile to be readily formed. The final product is

strong and durable. These eminently practical materials find applications from ball bearings to metal sheets formed into automobile bodies. An interesting class of alloys known as high strength low alloy (HSLA) steels has emerged in response to requirements for weight reduction of vehicles.[4] The composition of many commercial HSLA steels are proprietary and specified by mechanical properties rather than composition. The strength of HSLA steels is the result of optimal alloy selection and carefully controlled processing such as hot rolling.

(2) Stainless steels and tool steels are two general kinds of high alloy steels. Stainless steel is a term used to describe high Cr and Ni-Cr steels. The amount of Cr is at least 4 wt% and usually above 10 wt%. These steels are used to resist high temperatures and corrosive atmospheres. Some high Cr steels can be hardened by heat treatment and are used to resist abrasion and corrosion. Typical applications are plastic injection molds because the high Cr content allows the steel to be highly polished and prevents deterioration of cavity from heat and corrosion.[5] Tool steels are used for cutting, forming or otherwise shaping another material. The main alloying elements used in tool steels are tungsten, chromium and molybdenum. Their advantage is that they can provide the necessary hardness with simple heat treatments and retain that hardness at higher operating temperature.

durable 持久的，耐用的
ball bearing 球轴承
metal sheet 金属板材
HSLA 低合金高强度钢

commercial 商业的
proprietary 专有的
optimal 最佳的
hot rolling 热轧

stainless steels 不锈钢
tool steels 工具钢

Notes

1. This represents an immense family of engineering materials with a wide range of microstructures and related properties.

钢铁是工程材料中的一个巨大家族，它们的微观结构差别很大，并且具有相互关联的特性。

句首的 This 指代前句的 ferrous alloys。

2. The majority of engineering designs that require structural load support or power transmission involve ferrous alloys.

多数要求结构有一定的承载力或传输动力的工程设计都会涉及到钢铁。

that require structural…transmission 为 engineering designs 的定语从句。

3. Low carbon steels are well suited for the following applications: tool bodies, handles, die shoes and similar situations where strength and wear resistance are not required.

低碳钢适合用在以下应用中：刀具体、手柄、模座以及类似的没有强度和耐磨性要求的应用。

where strength and wear resistance are not required 为 situations 的定语从句。

4. An interesting class of alloys known as high strength low alloy (HSLA) steels has emerged in response to requirements for weight reduction of vehicles.

一类有趣的合金钢——低合金刚强度钢是为了满足降低汽车重量的要求而产生的。

in response to 意为"响应，反应"。

5. Typical applications are plastic injection molds because the high Cr content allows the steel to be highly polished and prevents deterioration of cavity from heat and corrosion.

(不锈钢)的典型应用就是塑料注射模具，因为高的含铬量使得这种钢材可以被高度抛光并且能防止由于高温和腐蚀造成的型腔磨损。

介词 from 在此为"由于"的意思。例如，She was nearly crying from the pain of her cut leg. 割破腿的疼痛使得她几乎要哭了。

 New Words and Expressions

represent [repri'zent] *vt.* 代表，扮演
immense [i'mens] *adj.* 极大的，巨大的
microstructure ['maikrəu'strʌktʃə] *n.* 微观结构
power ['pauə] *n.* 动力，功率，能力，权力
transmission [trænz'miʃən] *n.* 传送，传输
involve [in'vɔlv] *v.* 包括，涉及，牵涉
composition [kɔmpə'ziʃən] *n.* 成分；合成物
machine [mə'ʃi:n] *n.* 机器 *v.* 机加工
weld [weld] *v.* 焊接
harden ['hɑ:dn] *v.* (使)变硬
case hardening 表面淬火
stud [stʌd] *n.* 柱头螺栓，销子
pin [pin] *n.* 销，栓
axle ['æksl] *n.* 轴，心棒，车(轮)轴，轴线
nut [nʌt] *n.* 螺母，螺帽，坚果，难解的问题
moderately ['mɔdəritli] *adv.* 适度地，中等地
absence ['æbsəns] *n.* 缺乏，缺席
durable ['djuərəbl] *adj.* 持久的，耐用的
eminently ['eminəntli] *adv.* 不寻常地
ball bearing 球轴承
metal sheet 金属板材
vehicle ['vi:ikl] *n.* 交通工具，车辆

frequently ['fri:kwəntli] *adv.* 时常，往往
drill bushing 钻套
locator [ləu'keitə] *n.* 定位件，定位器
wear pad 耐磨垫
chromium ['krəumjəm] *n.* 铬(Cr)
nickel ['nikl] *n.* 镍(Ni)
tungsten ['tʌŋstən] *n.* 钨(W)
manganese ['mæŋgəni:z] *n.* 锰(Mn)
vanadium [və'neidiəm] *n.* 钒(V)
molybdenum [mə'libdinəm] *n.* 钼(Mo)
corrosion [kə'rəuʒən] *n.* 腐蚀，侵蚀
corrosion resistance 耐腐蚀性
invariably [in'vɛəriəb(ə)li] *adv.* 不变地，总是
arbitrary ['ɑ:bitrəri] *adj.* 武断的，独裁的
boundary ['baundəri] *n.* 边界，分界线
stainless steels 不锈钢
tool steels 工具钢
corrosive [kə'rəusiv] *adj.* 腐蚀性的
abrasion [ə'breiʒən] *n.* 磨损
injection molds 注射模
polish ['pɔliʃ] *v.* 抛光，擦亮，磨光，推敲
cavity ['kæviti] *n.* 型腔，洞，空穴

commercial [kəˈməːʃəl] adj. 商业的，贸易的
proprietary [prəˈpraiətəri] adj. 专利的，独占的
specified [ˈspesifaid] adj. 规定的，精确确定的
optimal [ˈɔptiməl] adj. 最佳的，最理想的
hot rolling 热轧

deterioration [di,tiəriəˈreiʃən] n. 磨损，退化
shape [ʃeip] v. 使成形，形成 n. 外形，形状
retain [riˈtein] v. 保持，保留
as a practical matter 实用中，实际上
fall into 可分成；陷入；开始；流入

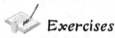
Exercises

I. Complete the following sentences according to the text.

1. There are two general kinds of steels: _____ and _____.

2. As the _____ _____ is increased in carbon steel, the strength, _____, and _____ are also increased when the metal is _____ _____.

3. The additional elements make essential _____ in the steels' properties such as higher _____ or improved _____ resistance.

4. Stainless steel is a term used to describe high _____ and _____ steels.

5. The strength of HSLA steels is the result of optimal _____ _____ and carefully controlled processing such as _____ _____.

II. Translate the following phrases into Chinese or English.

1. 承 载 _____ 2. 中碳钢 _____ 3. 模座 _____
4. 机加工 _____ 5. 不锈钢 _____ 6. 型腔 _____
7. 动力传递 _____ 8. 表面淬火 _____ 9. hot rolling _____
10. 耐腐蚀性 _____ 11. ball bearing _____ 12. metal sheet _____

III. Translate the following sentences into Chinese.

1. As the carbon content is increased in carbon steel, the strength, toughness and hardness are also increased when the metal is heat treated.

2. The final product is strong and durable. These eminently practical materials find applications from ball bearings to metal sheets formed into automobile bodies.

3. Their advantage is that they can provide the necessary hardness with simple heat treatments and retain that hardness at higher operating temperature.

Task 1.4　Cast Iron

As mentioned previously, we defined cast iron as the ferrous alloys with greater than 2 wt% carbon. They also generally contain up to 3 wt% silicon for control of carbide formation kinetics. Cast irons have relatively low melting temperature and liquid viscosities, do not form undesirable surface films when poured,

kinetics 动力学

viscosity 粘滞性

and undergo moderate shrinkage during solidification and cooling. The cast iron must balance good formability of complex shapes against inferior mechanical properties compared to wrought alloys.[1]

A cast iron is formed into a final shape by pouring molten metal into a mold. The shape of the mold is retained by the solidified metal. Inferior mechanical properties result from a less uniform microstructure, including some porosity. Wrought alloys are initially cast but are rolled or forged into final, relatively simple shapes. (in fact, "wrought" simply means "worked".)

Cast irons have four general types. White iron has a characteristic white, crystalline fracture surface. Large amounts of Fe_3C are formed during casting, giving a hard, brittle material. Gray iron has a gray fracture surface with a finely faceted structure. A significant silicon content(2 wt% to 3 wt%) promote graphite(C)precipitation rather than cementite(Fe_3C).[2] The sharp, pointed graphite flakes contribute to characteristic brittleness in gray iron. By adding a small amount(0.05 wt%)of Mg to the molten metal of the gray iron composition, spheroidal graphite precipitates rather than flakes are produced. Ductility is increased by a factor of 20, and strength is doubled. A more traditional form of cast iron with reasonable ductility is malleable iron, which is first cast as white iron and then heat treated to produce nodular graphite precipitates.[3]

shrinkage 收缩

inferior 下等的，次的
wrought alloys 可锻金属

uniform 统一的，均衡的
porosity 气孔，松孔
worked 被加工过的
white iron 白口铸铁
crystalline 结晶体的

fracture surface 断口面

gray iron 灰铸铁
promote 促进，提升
graphite 石墨
spheroidal 类似球体的
precipitate 沉积物，析出
factor 因数，倍
malleable iron 可锻铸铁
nodular 小瘤的，小结的

Notes

1. The cast iron must balance good formability of complex shapes against inferior mechanical properties compared to wrought alloys.

铸铁必须在复杂形状的良好成型性和与可锻金属而言相比较差的机械性能之间找到一个平衡点。

动词 balance 意为"权衡，平衡"。例如，You have to balance the advantages of living downtown against the disadvantages.——你必须权衡住在市中心的利弊。

2. A significant silicon content(2 wt% to 3 wt%)promote graphite(C)precipitation rather than cementite (Fe_3C).

硅的质量百分比达到2%～3%时，可显著促进石墨的析出，抑制渗碳体(Fe_3C)的形成。

3. A more traditional form of cast iron with reasonable ductility is malleable iron, which is first cast as white iron and then heat treated to produce nodular graphite precipitates.

可锻铸铁是一种更传统的、具有较好韧性的铸铁。它最初被浇注成白口铸铁，然后通过热处理析出小球状的石墨。

后半句 which is first cast…nodular graphite precipitates 为 malleable iron 的非限制性定语从句，可译成两个独立的句子。

New Words and Expressions

carbide [ˈkɑːbaid] n. 碳化物
kinetics [kaiˈnetiks] n. 动力学
viscosity [visˈkɔsiti] n. 粘滞性，粘度
film [film] n. 薄膜，薄皮；胶卷，影片
shrinkage [ˈʃrinkidʒ] n. 收缩，收缩量
inferior [inˈfiəriə] adj. 下级的，差的
uniform [ˈjuːnifɔːm] adj. 一致的，均衡的
porosity [pɔːˈrɔsiti] n. 气孔，松孔
forge [fɔːdʒ] v. 锻造
crystalline [ˈkristəlain] adj. 结晶体的
fracture surface 断口面
faceted [ˈfæsitid] adj. 有小平面的，有刻面的

promote [prəˈməut] v. 促进，提升
graphite [ˈɡræfait] n. 石墨
cementite [siˈmentait] n. 渗碳体，碳化铁
spheroidal [ˈsfiərɔidəl] adj. 类似球体的
precipitate [priˈsipiteit] v. & n. 沉积(物)，析出
precipitation [pri,sipiˈteiʃən] n. 沉积，凝结
factor [ˈfæktə] n. 因数，倍
nodular [ˈnɔdjulə(r)] adj. 小瘤的，小结的
white iron 白口铸铁
gray iron 灰铸铁
ductile iron 球墨铸铁(nodular graphite iron)
malleable iron 可锻铸铁

Exercises

Answer the following questions according to the text.

1. What are the casting properties of cast iron?
2. How many general types of cast iron are there? What are they?
3. What is the function of the element of Mg when it is added into the cast iron?
4. What is the shape of graphite precipitates in ductile iron?
5. How do we produce malleable iron?

Task 1.5　Polymers

　　Polymers are chemical compounds that consist of long, chainlike molecules made up of multiple repeating units. Metals, ceramics, and glasses are inorganic materials. The polymers discussed here are organic. The term polymer was coined in 1832 by the Swedish chemist Jims Berzelius from the the Greek: *poly* meaning "many" and *mer* meaning "part". Polymers are also referred to as "macromolecules", or "giant molecules" ── a term

polymer 聚合物
molecule 分子
multiple 多重的，若干
organic 有机的

giant 庞大的，巨大的

introduced by the German chemist Hermann Staudinger in 1922.

As important materials, the polymers are available in a wide variety of commercial forms: fibers, thin films and sheets, foams and in bulk. A common synonym for polymers is "plastic", a name derived from the deformability associated with the fabrication of most polymeric products.[1] Today, however, "plastic" is identified with the products which are derived from synthetic resins. The synthetic resins are made by various chemical processes.

Polymerization is the process by which long chain or network molecules are made from relatively small organic molecules. The structural features of the resulting polymers are rather unique compared to the inorganic materials. In general, the melting point and rigidity of polymers increase with extent of polymerization and with complexity of the molecular structure.[2]

Polymers or plastics fall into two main categories: thermosetting and thermoplastic. Upon the application of initial heat the thermosetting plastics soften and melt, and under pressure they will fill every crevice of a mold cavity. Upon continued application of heat they polymerize, or undergo a chemical change, which hardens them into a permanently hard, infusible, and insoluble state.[3] After this they cannot again be softened or melted by further heating. The thermoplastic materials are those which soften with heating and solidify and harden with cooling. They can be remelted and cooled time after time without undergoing any appreciable chemical change.

Plastics often contain other added materials called fillers. Fillers are employed to increase bulk and to help impart desired properties. Plastics containing fillers will cure faster and hold closer to established finished dimensions, since the plastic shrinkage will be reduced.[4] Wood flour is the general-purpose and most commonly used filler. Cotton frock, produced from cotton linters, increases mechanical strength. For higher strength and resistance to impact, cotton cloth chopped into sections about 1/2-inch square can be processed with the plastic. Asbestos fiber may be used as a filler for increased heat and fire resistance, and mica is used for molding plastic parts with superior dielectric characteristics. Glass fibers, silicon, cellulose, clay, or nutshell flour may also be used. Nutshell flour is used instead of wood flour where a better finish is desired. Plastic parts using short fiber fillers will result in lower costs, while those with long fiber fillers having greater impact strengths are more expensive. Other materials, not defined as fillers, such as dyes,

foam 泡沫
bulk 块
synonym 同义词
fabrication 制作，构成
synthetic 合成的

polymerization 聚合

inorganic 无机的
extent 程度

thermosetting 热固性
thermoplastic 热塑性

crevice 缺口，裂缝
infusible 不熔化的
insoluble 不能溶解的

appreciable 一点儿的

filler 填充物
impart 给予，传授
cure 凝固
hold 占据
general-purpose 多种用途的，多方面的
cotton frock 棉籽壳
cotton linter 轧棉机
asbestos 石棉
mica 云母
dielectric 绝缘体
cellulose 纤维素
clay 粘土，泥土

dye 染料

pigments, lubricants, accelerators, and plasticizers may also be added. Plasticizers are added to soften and improve the moldability of plastics. Filler and modifying agents are added and mixed with the raw plastic before it is molded or formed.

pigment 颜料
lubricant 润滑剂
accelerator 催化剂
plasticizer 塑化剂

Numerous plastics have already been discovered and developed by the chemists and chemical engineers, research on the synthetic resins is one of the most prominent fields in organic chemistry today.

prominent 杰出的，重要的

Notes

1. A common synonym for polymers is "plastic", a name derived from the deformability associated with the fabrication of most polymeric products.

"塑料"是聚合物的一个普通的同义词，这个名字源于与多数聚合物产品的制造过程紧密联系的可塑性。

a name derived … products 是一个双重过去分词结构，其中 derived … products 修饰 a name，associated with … products 修饰 the deformability。

2. In general, the melting point and rigidity of polymers increase with extent of polymerization and with complexity of the molecular structure.

通常，聚合物的熔点和硬度会随着聚合程度以及分子结构的复杂程度而增长。

3. Upon continued application of heat they polymerize, or undergo a chemical change, which hardens them into a permanently hard, infusible, and insoluble state.

当继续加热时，热固性塑料发生聚合，即发生化学变化，这使得热固性塑料发硬至永久硬化、很难熔化及很难溶解的状态。

4. Plastics containing fillers will cure faster and hold closer to established finished dimensions, since the plastic shrinkage will be reduced.

含有填充物的塑料凝固得更快，并且能更加接近已制定的最终尺寸，原因在于填充物可使塑料的收缩率下降。

现在分词短语 containing fillers 后置修饰 Plastics；连词 since 引导原因状语从句。

New Words and Expressions

polymer [ˈpɔlimə] n. 聚合物，聚合体
polymeric [ˌpɔliˈmerik] adj. 聚合的，聚合体的
polymerize [ˈpɔliməraiz] v. (使)聚合
polymerization [ˌpɔliməraiˈzeiʃən] n. 聚合
molecule [ˈmɔlikjuːl] n. 分子
multiple [ˈmʌltipl] adj. 多重的，若干
inorganic [ˌinɔːˈɡænik] adj. 无机的
organic [ɔːˈɡænik] adj. 有机的

rigidity [riˈdʒiditi] n. 刚性，硬度；刚直，严格
extent [iksˈtent] n. 范围，程度
thermosetting [ˌθəːməuˈsetiŋ] adj. 热固性的
thermoplastic [ˌθəːməˈplæstik] adj. 热塑性的
initial [iˈniʃəl] adj. 开始的，最初的
crevice [ˈkrevis] n. 缺口，裂缝
cotton frock 棉籽壳

Project 1　Foundations of Mechanics

coin [kɔin] v. 造字，杜撰新词语
giant ['dʒaiənt] adj. 庞大的，巨大的
foam [fəum] n. 泡沫
bulk [bʌlk] n. 块
synonym ['sinənim] n. 同义词
derive [di'raiv] v. 源自，出自
deformability [difɔ:mə'biliti] n. 可塑性
fabrication [,fæbri'keiʃən] n. 制造，生产
identify [ai'dentifai] v. 认为一致；鉴别
synthetic [sin'θetik] adj. 人造的，综合的
utilize [ju:'tilaiz] v. 利用
infusible [in'fju:zəbl] adj. 难熔化的
insoluble [in'sɔljubl] adj. 难溶解的
remelt ['ri:'melt] v. 再融化，再熔化
appreciable [ə'pri:ʃiəbl] adj. 一点儿,可感知的
filler ['filə] n. 填充物
impart [im'pɑ:t] v. 给予，传授，告知
cure [kjuə] v. 硬化，凝固

cotton linter 轧棉机
impact ['impækt] v. & n. 碰撞，冲击
chop [tʃɔp] v. & n. 切细；剁碎
asbestos [æz'bestɔs] n. 石棉
mica ['maikə] n. 云母
dielectric [,daii'lektrik] n. 绝缘体
clay [klei] n. 粘土，泥土
dye [dai] n. 染料，染色
pigment ['pigmənt] n. 色素，颜料
lubricant ['lu:brikənt] n. 润滑剂
accelerator [æk'seləreitə] n. 催化剂
plasticizer ['plæstisaizə] n. 塑化剂,增塑剂
modify ['mɔdifai] v. 更改，修改
agent ['eidʒənt] n. 药剂
prominent ['prɔminənt] adj. 杰出的，重要的
general-purpose 多种用途的，多方面的
cellulose nitrate 硝酸纤维
polyester resin 酚醛树脂
phenol formaldehyde resin 聚酯树脂

Exercises

I. Complete the following sentences according to the text.

1. Polymers are chemical _____ that consist of long, _____ _____ made up of multiple repeating units.

2. A common synonym for polymers is _____, a name derived from the _____ associated with the fabrication of most polymeric products.

3. _____ can be _____ and cooled time after time without undergoing any appreciable _____ change.

4. Plastics containing _____ will _____ faster and hold _____ to established _____ dimensions, since the plastic _____ will be reduced.

5. Asbestos _____ may be used as a filler for increased heat and _____ _____, and mica is used for _____ plastic parts with superior _____ characteristics.

II. Translate the following phrases into Chinese or English.

1. 冲击强度 _____　　2. 有机化学 _____　　3. 收缩率 _____
4. 调节剂，修改剂 _____　　5. general-purpose _____　　6. thermosetting _____
7. thermoplastic _____　　8. synthetic resin _____　　9. molecule _____

III. Translate the following passage into Chinese.

Polymers are complex and giant molecules and are different from low molecular compounds, like say, common salt. To contrast the difference, the molecular weight of common salt is only 58.5, while that of a polymer can be as high as several hundred thousands, even more than thousand thousands. Another striking difference between polymers and low molecular compounds is the dissolution process. That the long time taken by most polymers for dissolution, the absence of a saturation point, and the increase in the viscosity are all characteristics of a typical polymer being dissolved in a solvent.

Task 1.6 Heat Treatment of Steel

The role of heat treatment in modern mechanical engineering cannot be overestimated. The purpose of heat treatment is to control the properties of a metal through the alteration of the structure of the metal by heating it to definite temperatures and cooling at various rates. This combination of heating and controlled cooling determines not only the nature and distribution of the microconstituents, which in turn determine the properties, but also the grain size.[1] The changes in the properties of metals due to heat treatment are of extremely great significance.

Heat treatment conditions' characteristics parameters are: heating temperature, time of holding at the heating temperature, heating rate, and cooling rate. In general, the rate of cooling is the controlling factor, rapid cooling from above the critical range results in hard structure, whereas very slow cooling produces the opposite effect. Heat treatment of ferrous materials involves several important operations which are customarily referred to under various names, such as normalizing, annealing, hardening, tempering, case hardening, spheroidizing, and stress relieving.

The primary purpose of ***annealing*** is to soften hard steel so that it may be machined or cold worked. Full annealing is usually accomplished by heating the steel to slightly above the critical temperature, holding it there until the temperature of the piece is uniform throughout, and then cooling at a slowly controlled rate so that the temperature of the surface and that of the center are approximately the same. This process wipes out all trace of previous structure, refines the crystalline structure, and softens the metal. Annealing also relieves internal stresses previously set up in the metal. Annealing may not be the most suitable treatment for low carbon

overestimate 过高评价
alteration 改变，变更

distribution 分布，分发
grain 晶粒

significance 意义
parameter 参数，参量

critical 临界的，批判的

customarily 通常

spheroidizing 球化处理
stress relieving 去应力
annealing 退火
accomplish 完成，实现

approximately 大约
refine 精炼，细化
internal 内部的

steels, which after fully annealed are too soft and relatively weak, offering little resistance to cutting, but usually having sufficient ductility and toughness that a cut chip tends to pull and tear the finished surface, leaving a comparatively poor surface quality that results in a poor machinability.[2] However, the machinability of most of high carbon steels and alloy steels can usually be greatly improved by annealing, as they are often too hard and strong to be easily cut at any but their softest condition. Tool steel is generally purchased in the annealed condition. Sometimes it is necessary to rework a tool that has been hardened, and the tool must then be annealed. For maximum softness and ductility the cooling rate should be as slow as allowing the parts to cool down with the furnace. The higher the carbon content, the slower cooling rate must be.

The purpose of *normalizing* is usually to refine grain structure that has been coarsened in forging. With most of the medium carbon forging steels, alloyed and unalloyed, normalizing is highly recommended after forging and before machining to produce more homogeneous structures, and in most cases, improved machinability.[3] Most commercial steels are normalized after rolled and cast. But high alloy air-hardened steels are never normalized, since to do so would cause them to harden and defeat the primary purpose. Normalizing involves heating the metal to a temperature of about 55~100℃ above the critical range and cooling in still air.

Hardening, also called quenching, is the oldest and most effective process to harden metals, whose purpose is to produce martensite. The four common cooling mediums, arranged in order of decreasing cooling ability, are the following: brine, water, light and heave oil, and air. High temperature gradients contribute to high stresses that cause distortion and cracking, so the quenching only produces the necessary desired structure. Care must be exercised in quenching that heat is removed uniformly to minimize thermal stresses. Two special types of quenching are conducted to minimize quenching stresses and decrease the tendency for distortion and cracking. In both, the steel is quenched in a salt bath held at a selected lower temperature before being allowed to cool. These processes, known as *austempering* and *martempering*, result in products having certain desired physical properties.

Steel that has been hardened by rapid quenching is brittle and not suitable for most use. By ***tempering***, the hardness and brittleness may be reduced to the desired point for service conditions. As these properties are reduced there is also a decrease in tensile strength and an increase in the ductility and toughness of the steel. Although this process softens steel, it differs considerably from annealing in that the process lends itself to close control of the physical properties and in most cases dose not soften the steel to the extent that annealing would.[4] The final structure obtained from tempering a fully hardened steel is called tempered martensite. The magnitude of the structural changes and the change of properties caused by tempering depend upon the temperature to which the steel is reheated. The higher the temperature, the greater the effect, so the choice of temperature will generally depend on willingness to sacrifice hardness and strength to gain ductility and toughness.

The addition of carbon to the surface of steel parts and the subsequent hardening operations are important processes in heat treating, called ***case hardening***. The process may involve the use of molten sodium cyanide mixture, pack carburizing with activated solid materials such as charcoal or coke, gas or oil carburizing, and dry cyaniding.

tempering 回火

tensile strength 抗拉强度

sacrifice 牺牲

subsequent 后来的

sodium cyanide 氰化钠
carburizing 渗碳剂
activated 有活性的

Notes

1. This combination of heating and controlled cooling determines not only the nature and distribution of the microconstituents, which in turn determine the properties, but also the grain size.

将加热和可控制的冷却相结合，不仅可以决定微观组织的性质和分布，还可以决定晶粒的大小。其中，微观组织的性质和分布又可以决定材料的性能。

2. Annealing may not be the most suitable treatment for low carbon steels, which after fully annealed are too soft and relatively weak, offering little resistance to cutting, but usually having so sufficient ductility and toughness that a cut chip tends to pull and tear the finished surface, leaving a comparatively poor surface quality that results in a poor machinability.

退火并不是最适合低碳钢的热处理方法。经过完全退火的低碳钢硬度过低，强度也相对小，使得其对切削的阻力小，但是由于其有足够的塑性和韧性，切屑时会拉伤和磨损已加工表面，使表面质量变差，因此切削加工性差。

which 至句末是非限制性定语从句，修饰 low carbon steels。在这个从句中，offering…、having…和 leaving…是 3 个递进关系的现在分词短语作结果状语；having…中是 so…that 句型，leaving…中 that 引导的定语从句修饰 a comparatively poor surface quality。

3. With most of the medium carbon forging steels, alloyed and unalloyed, normalizing is

highly recommended after forging and before machining to produce more homogeneous structures, and in most cases, improved machinability.

对于多数中碳钢，无论是否在其中加入合金，极力推荐在其锻造后和机械加工前进行正火处理，从而产生更为均匀的组织，而且在多数情况下还可改善切削加工性。

4. Although this process softens steel, it differs considerably from annealing in that the process lends itself to close control of the physical properties and in most cases dose not soften the steel to the extent that annealing would.

尽管(回火)这种方法也可将钢软化，但它与退火有很大差别，因为(回火)这种方法适于精确地控制材料的物理性能，而且在多数情况下回火钢没有退火钢那么软。

"in that…annealing would."是由 in that 引导的原因状语从句，说明回火和退火之间的的两个差异。

in that 意思为"因为"，lend itself to 为习惯用法，意思为"适合于……"。

New Words and Expressions

overestimate [ˌəuvəˈestimeit] v. 过高评价
alteration [ˌɔːltəˈreiʃən] n. 改变，变更
distribution [ˌdistriˈbjuːʃən] n. 分布，分发
constituent [kənˈstitjuənt] n. & adj. 要素，组分
microconstituent 微观组织，微观成分
grain [grein] n. 晶粒，谷物，细粒
significance [sigˈnifikəns] n. 意义，重要性
parameter [pəˈræmitə] n. 参数，参量
critical [ˈkritikəl] adj. 临界的，批判的
customarily [ˈkʌstəmərili] adv. 通常
spheroidizing [ˈsfiərɔidaiziŋ] n. 球化处理
stress relieving 去应力
annealing [æˈniːliŋ] n. 退火
accomplish [əˈkɔmpliʃ] v. 完成，实现
approximately [əprɔksiˈmətli] adv. 大约
refine [riˈfain] v. 精炼，细化
internal [inˈtəːnl] adj. 内部的
machinability [məʃiːnəˈbiliti] n. 切削加工性
purchase [ˈpəːtʃəs] v. 购买
normalizing [ˈnɔːməlaiziŋ] n. 正火
coarsen [ˈkɔːsn] v. 变粗糙
recommend [rekəˈmend] v. 推荐
homogeneous [hɔmeuˈdʒiːnjəs] adj. 均匀的

primary [ˈpraiməri] adj. 最初的，主要的
still [stil] adj. 静止的
quenching [ˈkwentʃiŋ] n. 淬火
martensite [ˈmɑːtənzait] n. 马氏体
medium [ˈmiːdiəm] n. 媒介 adj. 中间的
brine [brain] n. 盐溶液
gradient [ˈgreidiənt] n. 变化率，坡度，梯度
distortion [disˈtɔːʃən] n. 扭曲，变形，曲解
cracking [ˈkrækiŋ] n. 开裂，裂缝，裂痕
tendency [ˈtendənsi] n. 倾向，趋向
salt bath 盐浴(炉，槽)
austempering [ɔːsˈtempəriŋ] n. 等温淬火
martempering [ˈmɑːˌtempəriŋ] n. 分级淬火
tempering [ˈtempəriŋ] n. 回火
tensile [ˈtensail] adj. 可拉长的，拉力的
tensile strength 抗拉强度
sacrifice [ˈsækrifais] n. & v. 牺牲，献出
subsequent [ˈsʌbsikwənt] adj. 随后的，后来的
sodium [ˈsəudjəm] n. 钠
cyanide [ˈsaiənaid] n. 氰化物
dry cyaniding 干法氰化
carburizing [ˈkɑːbjuraiziŋ] n. 渗碳剂
activated [ˈæktiveitid] adj. 有活性的

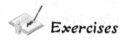 **Exercises**

I. Complete the following sentences according to the text.

1. The purpose of heat treatment is to control the _____ of a metal through the alteration of the _____ of the metal by _____ it to definite temperatures and _____ at various rates.

2. Heat treatment of ferrous materials involves several important operations which are customarily referred to under various names, such as _____, _____, _____, _____, _____, spheroidizing, and stress relieving.

3. Annealing _____ out all _____ of previous structure, _____ the crystalline structure, and _____ the metal.

4. High _____ gradients in hardening contribute to _____ that cause _____ and _____, so the quenching only produces the necessary desired structure.

5. Steel that has been _____ by rapid quenching is _____ and not suitable for most use. By _____, the _____ and brittleness may be _____ to the desired point for service conditions.

II. Translate the following phrases into Chinese or English.

1. 冷却速度 _____   2. 冷却介质 _____   3. 冷加工 _____
4. 晶粒尺寸 _____   5. 表面质量 _____   6. 内应力 _____
7. 变形 _____   8. 开裂 _____   9. 临界温度 _____
10. 切削加工性 _____ 11. 切屑 _____   12. 活性材料 _____
13. annealing _____ 14. normalizing _____ 15. hardening(quenching) _____
16. tempering _____ 17. case hardening _____ 18. packing carburizing _____
19. tensile strength _____ 20. tempered martensite _____ 21. ductility _____

III. Translate the following sentences into Chinese.

1. The principal kinds of heat treatment used in practice, which differently affect the structure and properties, and which are assigned to meet the requirements made to semifabricated materials (castings, forgings, rolled stock, etc.)and finished articles, are : annealing, normalizing, hardening and tempering.

2. Normalizing raises the strength and hardness of medium and high carbon steels by 10 to 15 percent as compared to annealed steel.

3. When such a quenched steel is tempered, structures with mechanical properties intermediate between those of the slowly cooled and the quenched conditions are formed.

IV. Translate the following passage into Chinese.

In the die casting industry surface treatments are applied to steels to improve the properties of nozzles, ejector pins, cores and shot sleeves, to provide maximum resistance to erosion, pitting and soldering. Treatment of die cavities has received only limited acclaim, because the complex thermal patterns produced on large die components lead to premature failure. Experience in drop forging has also indicated that surface treatments of their dies have not been particularly successful.

Thermochemaical treatments are applied to die casting and die components. The surface chemistry of the steel is modified by the introduction of nitrogen, carbon and sometimes other elements. The processes are of the main types listed below: nitriding, nitrocarburizing such as tufftride and sulfinuzing, metalizing such as boronizing and the Toyota diffusion process, carburizing and carbonitriding.

Task 1.7　Die Materials

A set of die may contain 10 or more different steels plus several non-ferrous metals and special heat resisting alloys.[1]

Parts of the die which merely act as bearings can be made of non-ferrous metals such as phosphor bronze, or medium carbon steel.

The mechanisms for moving the ejectors and cores must work smoothly in the constantly changing temperature of a die. The box sections, ejector plates and sprue puller are made of mild steel, with about 0.15% carbon. The guide pillars and ejector stops, which are to support and guide the die, and endure shock loading, are made of case hardened mild steel; occasionally case hardened nickel steels are used for increasing strength[2]. Bolsters undergo mechanical impact and stress but not a great deal of thermal shock and are often made of medium carbon steel; alternatively these parts are steel castings or they may be of a spheroidal graphite cast iron. Normally the bushes are made of carburized steel.

The die blocks are usually made of medium carbon steel, whose typical British specification is BS970 08M40 (En8), with 0.4% carbon, 0.8% manganese and 0.3% silicon. Sometimes a prehardened steel is used, with 0.35% carbon, 10% manganese, 0.5% silicon, 1.65% chromium and 0.5% molybdenum. This composition is covered by the American AISI specification P.20.

The die inserts, the cores and the cavities, which have to withstand the impact and high temperature of the molten material, are made of alloy steel given a nitride or other treatment to resist wear and heat.

phosphor bronze 磷青铜

mechanism 机构
ejector 顶料或推件设备
core 型芯
sprue puller 拉料杆

mild steel 低碳钢
guide pillar 导柱
ejector stop 止推设备
bolster 垫板

carburize 渗碳
die block 模座，凹凸模固定板

preharden 预硬化

specification 规范，标准
insert 嵌件，入子
cavity 型腔

Notes

1. A set of die may contain 10 or more different steels plus several non-ferrous metals and special heat resisting alloys.

一副模具可能含有 10 多种钢，以及一些有色金属和特种耐热合金。

2. The guide pillars and ejector stops, which are to support and guide the die, and endure shock loading, are made of case hardened mild steel; occasionally case hardened nickel steels are used for increasing strength.

支承和引导模具，以及承受冲击载荷的导柱和止推设备由低碳钢经表面硬化制成。有时为了获得更大的强度也用镍钢经表面硬化制成。

New Words and Expressions

phosphor ['fɔsfə] n. 磷(P)
bronze [brɔnz] n. 青铜
mechanism ['mekənizəm] n. 机构，机制
ejector [i'dʒektə] n. 顶料或推件设备，排出器
core [kɔ:] n. 型芯
sprue [spru:] n. 浇口，直浇道，主流道
pillar ['pilə] n. 柱子，栋梁
bolster ['bəulstə] n. 垫板，支撑板
carburize ['kɑ:bjuraiz] v. 渗碳

preharden 预硬化
specification [ˌspesifi'keiʃən] n. 规范，说明书
insert [in'sə:t] n. 嵌件，入子
cavity ['kæviti] n. 型腔
spheroidal ['sfiərɔidəl] adj. 类似球体的
graphite ['græfait] n. 石墨
spheroidal graphite cast iron 球墨铸铁
die block 模座，凹凸模固定板
mild steel 低碳钢

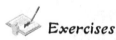

I. Translate the following phrases into Chinese or English.

1. 型　芯 _____ 2. 型　腔 _____ 3. 嵌　件 _____
4. 导　柱 _____ 5. 模　座 _____ 6. 低碳钢 _____
7. 排出器 _____ 8. 浇　口 _____

II. Translate the following sentences into Chinese.

1. The mechanisms for moving the ejectors and cores must work smoothly in the constantly changing temperature of a die.

2. The die inserts, the cores and the cavities, which have to withstand the impact and high temperature of the molten material, are made of alloy steel given a nitride or other treatment to resist wear and heat.

III. Question: Which materials are the die blocks usually made of?

Project 2

Forming Machines

Task 2.1　Presses

The press working process is to apply the large forces by press tools for a short time interval in order to produce the shearing or deformation of the work material. The time of producing a finished part is generally less than one second. Press working forces are set up, guided, and controlled in a machine referred to as a press. Energy stored in the rotating flywheel of a mechanical press or supplied by a hydraulic system in a hydraulic press is transferred to the ram for its linear movements.[1]

shearing 剪切，切割
deformation 变形

rotating 旋转的
hydraulic 液压的
ram 滑块，压头

Essentially, major components of a press are as follows: a bed, a bolster plate, a reciprocating part called a ram or slide which exerts forces upon work material through special tools mounted on the ram and bed, a knockout, and a cushion. The press bed is the rectangular part of the frame and is often open in its center, which supports the bolster plate. The steel bolster plate is often 50~130mm thick, upon which press tools and accessories are mounted. Bolsters having standard dimensions and openings are available from press manufactures. The ram or slide is the upper part that moves through a stroke, a distance depending on the size and design of the press. The position of the ram, but not the stroke, can be adjusted in most presses except hydraulic presses. The distance from the top of the bed(or bolster)to the bottom of the slide, with its stroke down and adjustment up, is the shut height of a press.[2] The knockout is the mechanism operating on the upstroke of a press, which ejects workpieces or blanks from a press tool. The cushion is

stroke 行程，冲程
bolster 工作台

shut height 闭合高度

eject 排出，喷出

the press accessory located beneath or within a bolster for producing an upward motion and force; it is actuated by air, oil, rubber, or springs or a combination of mechanisms.

  The following are the basic types used in industry.

  (1) An open-back inclinable press, also called a gap-frame press (Fig.2.1), has a C-shaped frame which can be inclined an angle to the base, allowing for the disposal of finished parts by gravity. The open back allows the feeding and unloading of stock, workpieces, and finished parts from front to back.

blank 边，空白处
actuate 驱动，促使
spring 弹簧

inclinable 可倾斜的

disposal 处理，安排

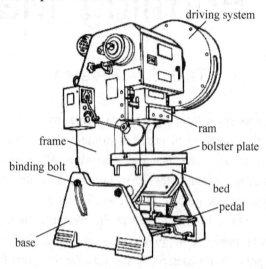

Fig. 2.1　Open-back inclinable press

  (2) A straight side press has columns at ends of the bed, with rectangular windows to allow the feeding and unloading of stock, workpieces.

column 立柱

  (3) A hydraulic press is extensively used in open-die forging, extrusion, and sheet metal forming. In addition, it may be used in wire drawing, powder metallurgy, plastic forming, and special forming. The ram of a hydraulic press is driven by hydraulic cylinders and pistons, which are parts of high pressure hydraulic or hydropneumatic system. After a rapid approach speed, the ram with upper die attached moves at a slow speed while exerting a squeezing force on the work metal. Pressing speeds can be accurately controlled to permit control of metal-flow velocities; this is particularly advantageous in producing close-tolerance forgings. And that the working pressure and the stroke can be adjusted is another advantage of a hydraulic press.

extrusion 挤压
drawing 拉拔，拉深
metallurgy 冶金
cylinder 缸
piston 活塞
pneumatic 气动的
exert 施加，发挥
squeeze 挤压
velocity 速度
close-tolerance 小公差

  (4) A double-action press is usually used for deep drawing

on sheet metal parts. This type of press has two mechanically actuated slides: a blank holder slide and a draw slide. The blank holder slide is hollow rectangular and is guided on gibs located on the press uprights. The draw slide fits into and moves up and down along the gibs of the hollow blank holder. Both slides are driven from a centralized drive including a single clutch and brake for actuation. In a typical press cycle, when the clutch is actuated, the blank holder descends faster than the draw slide. The blank holder contacts the stamping at about the time when the draw slide is halfway down on its stroke. The blank holder slide then dwells, or remains stationary under pressure, while the draw slide completes its down stroke. The blank holder holds the blank to prevent it from wrinkling.

(5) A triple-action press has the same inner and outer ram as the double-action press, but a third ram in the press bed moves up allowing a reverse draw to be made in one press cycle.[3]

(6) A knuckle press is used for coining. The drive design allows for very high pressures at the bottom of the ram stroke. This type uses a crank, which moves a joint consisting of two levers that oscillate to and from dead center and results in a short, powerful movement of the slide with slow travel near the bottom of the stroke.[4]

(7) A press brake is essentially the same as a gap-frame press except for its long bed from 1.8 to 2m or more. It is used mainly for bending operations on large sheet metal parts. It can also be used with a series of separate sets of press tools to do light piercing, notching, and forming. This allows parts of a complex design to be accurately made without a high-cost press tool by simply breaking the complex part down into several simple operations. This type of operation is used on low-run or prototype parts. The tooling cost is usually very low, but the labor cost is high as the parts are manually located and transferred in each station.

Press operator safety must be a primary concern for everyone in the press area. While working under the ram the press control must be locked in the "*Off*" position and safety blocks placed under the ram to prevent it from coasting down. While the press is running, the use of proper guards and safety procedures must always be followed.

a blank holder slide 压边滑块
a draw slide 冲压滑块
gib 导轨
upright 立柱
clutch 离合器
brake 闸
descend 下降

dwell 停顿
stationary 静止的
wrinkling 起皱

reverse 相反的
coining 压印，压花
crank 曲柄
oscillate 摆动，振荡
bending 弯曲
piercing 冲孔
notching 开槽
prototype 样品，模型
manually 手工地
transfer 移动，传递
concern 关注，关心
coasting 惯性运动
procedure 措施，方法

Notes

1. Energy stored in the rotating flywheel of a mechanical press or supplied by a hydraulic system in a hydraulic press is transferred to the ram for its linear movements.

存储在机械压力机的旋转飞轮中的能量或者由水压机的液压系统提供的能量被传递给滑块，从而产生滑块的直线运动。

stored in…a mechanical press 和 supplied by…a hydraulic press 是两个过去分词短语作后置定语，修饰 energy。

2. The distance from the top of the bed (or bolster) to the bottom of the slide, with its stroke down and adjustment up, is the shut height of a press.

从工作台顶端到滑块(滑块分别处于行程最低和回复至行程最高的两个位置)底部之间的距离，称为压力机的闭合高度。

from the top…to the bottom of the slide 是介词短语作后置定语，修饰 the distance。

with its stroke down and adjustment up 是一个伴随状语，说明测量距离时 the slide 的位置有两个：行程的最低和最高，即闭合高度是一个距离区间。

3. A triple-action press has the same inner and outer ram as the double-action press, but a third ram in the press bed moves up allowing a reverse draw to be made in one press cycle.

三动式压力机和双动式压力机一样也有内、外滑块，但它在工作台里还有另一个滑块，该滑块可向上运动，从而在一个冲压循环中产生反向拉伸。

在序数词 third 前使用不定冠词 a，主要侧重 another(另一个)的意思，不强调次序。

4. This type uses a crank, which moves a joint consisting of two levers that oscillate to and from dead center and results in a short, powerful movement of the slide with slow travel near the bottom of the stroke.

这种型号的压力机(肘式压力机)采用曲柄，该曲柄通过移动一个由两根在死点之间来回摆动的连杆构成的接头，从而使得滑块在冲程末端运行减慢，产生一个短且有力的运动。

which 至句末为非限制性定语从句，修饰 a crank。consisting of…dead center 为现在分词短语作后置定语，修饰 a joint，其中嵌入一个定语从句 that oscillate to and from dead center 修饰 two levers。

 New Words and Expressions

press [pres] *n. & v.* 压，挤压
        n. 压力机，冲床
interval [ˈintəvəl] *n.* 时间间隔
shearing [ˈʃiəriŋ] *n.* 剪切，切割
deformation [ˌdiːfɔːˈmeiʃən] *n.* 变形
rotating [rəuˈteitiŋ] *adj.* 旋转的
flywheel [ˈflaiwiːl] *n.* 飞轮，惯性轮，储能轮

a triple-action press 三动式压力机
shut height 闭合高度
eject [iˈdʒekt] *v.* 逐出，撵出，驱逐，喷射
locate [ləuˈkeit] *v.* 定位，放置
beneath [biˈniːθ] *prep. & adv.* 在……之下
actuate [ˈæktjueit] *v.* 驱动，开动，促使
spring [spriŋ] *n.* 弹簧；泉；春天

Project 2　Forming Machines

hydraulic [hai'drɔ:lik] adj. 液压的，水力的
hydraulic press 水压机，液压压力机
mechanical press 机械压力机，曲柄压力机
transfer [træns'fə:] n. & v. 移动，传递
linear ['liniə] adj. 直线的，线性的
ram [ræm] n. 滑块，活塞，压头
component [kəm'pəunənt] n. 元件，成分
bolster ['bəulstə] n. 垫子，台面，穿孔台
reciprocating [ri'siprəkeitiŋ] adj. 往复的
slide [slaid] n. 滑块，滑动装置
exert [ig'zə:t] v. 施加(压力等)，努力
mount [maunt] v. 装上，设置，安放
knockout ['nɔkaut] n. 打料装置，脱模机
cushion ['kuʃən] n. 软垫，缓冲垫，减震垫
rectangular [rek'tæŋgjulə] adj. 矩形的
frame [freim] n. 机架，框架
accessory [æk'sesəri] n. 附件，零件，附加物
opening ['əupəniŋ] n. 槽，空隙，口，孔
manufacture [,mænju'fæktʃə] n. 制造，工厂
mechanism ['mekənizəm] n. 机械装置，机构
stroke [strəuk] n. 行程，冲程；击，敲
adjust [ə'dʒʌst] v. 调整，调节，校准
adjustment [ə'dʒʌstmənt] n. 调整，调节
tolerance ['tɔlərəns] n. 公差，宽容，忍受
close-tolerance 小公差(的)
a double-action press 双动式压力机
contact ['kɔntækt] n. & v. 结出，联系
a blank holder slide 压边滑块
a draw slide 冲压滑块
hollow ['hɔləu] adj. 中空的，凹的
gib [gib] n. 凹字形楔，凹槽
upright ['ʌp'rait] n. 立柱
　　　　　　adj. 直立的，直立的
centralized ['sentrəlaizd] adj. 集中的
clutch [klʌtʃ] n. 离合器 v. 抓住，攫住
brake [breik] n. & v. 闸，刹车
drive [draiv] n. 驱动器，动力
descend [di'send] v. 下降
deep drawing 深拉深，深冲压
contact ['kɔntækt] n. & v. 接触，联系

combination [,kɔmbi'neiʃən] n. 组合，联合
incline [in'klain] n. & v. 倾斜，倾向，斜坡
inclinable [in'klainəbl] adj. 可倾斜的，倾向于
disposal [dis'pəuzəl] n. 处置，布置，安排
gravity ['græviti] n. 重力，地心引力
column ['kɔləm] n. 立柱；专栏；纵队
stock [stɔk] n. 原料；股票；树干；库存
extensively [iks'tensivli] adv. 广阔地
open-die forging 自由锻
extrusion [eks'tru:ʒən] n. 挤压，挤出，冲塞
sheet metal 钣金，金属板材
wire drawing 线材拉拔
powder ['paudə] n. 粉末；火药；尘土
metallurgy [me'tælədʒi] n. 冶金，冶金学
cylinder ['silində] n.(汽)缸，圆柱体，柱面
piston ['pistən] n. 活塞，柱塞
pneumatic [nju(:)'mætik] adj.气动的,风动的
hydropneumatic 液压气动的
approach [ə'prəutʃ] n. & v. 接近，靠近
attach [ə'tætʃ] v. 系上，贴上，隶属于
squeeze [skwi:z] n. & v. 挤压，压榨
velocity [vi'lɔsiti] n. 速度，速率
advantageous [,ædvən'teidʒəs] adj. 有利的
reverse [ri'və:s] n. & adj. 相反的 v. 颠倒
a knuckle press 肘式压力机
oscillate ['ɔsileit] v. 摆动，振荡
bottom ['bɔtəm] n. & adj. 底部的
crank [kræŋk] n. 曲柄
joint [dʒɔint] n. 节点，关节
lever ['li:və] n. 连杆，杠杆
coining ['kɔiniŋ] n. 压印，压花，模压，冲制
a press brake 压板机，压弯机
bending ['bendiŋ] n. 弯曲，挠度
piercing ['piəsiŋ] n. 冲孔，钻孔
notching ['nɔtʃiŋ] n. 开槽，做凹口
low-run 小批量
prototype ['prəutətaip] n. 样品，模型
manually ['mænjuəli] adv. 手工地
primary ['praiməri] adj. 最初的，首要的
concern [kən'sə:n] n. 关心，关注

stamping [ˈstæmpiŋ] *n. & v.* 冲压，冲压件(片)
dwell [dwel] *n. & v.* 停顿，停留，定居
stationary [ˈsteiʃ(ə)nəri] *adj.* 静止的
wrinkling [ˈriŋkliŋ] *n.* 起皱现象，起皱纹

coasting [ˈkəustiŋ] *n.* 惯性运动，惰力运转
safety blocks 安全块
procedure [prəˈsi:dʒə] *n.* 措施，行动，手续
guard [gɑ:d] *n.* 防护装置，守卫

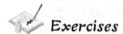

Exercises

I. Complete the following sentences according to the text.

1. The press working process is to apply the large _____ by press _____ for a short _____ _____ in order to produce the _____ or _____ of the work material.

2. While working under the ram the press control must be _____ in the "*Off*" position and safety blocks placed _____ the ram to prevent it from _____ down.

3. The _____ back allows the _____ and _____ of _____, workpieces, and finished parts from front to back.

4. Pressing _____ can be accurately controlled to permit control of _____ velocities; this is particularly advantageous in producing _____ _____.

5. A hydraulic press is extensively used in _____ _____, _____, and _____ _____ _____. In addition, it may be used in _____ _____, _____ metallurgy, plastic _____, and special forming.

II. Translate the following phrases into Chinese or English.

1. 冲孔 _____   2. 弯曲 _____   3. 拉深 _____   4. 印花 _____
5. 挤压 _____   6. 开槽 _____   7. 剪切 _____   8. 原料 _____
9. 小公差 _____ 10. 行程 _____ 11. 样品 _____ 12. 小批量 _____
13. hydraulic cylinder _____   14. open-die forging _____   15. accessory _____
16. upper die _____   17. sheet metal _____   18. approach speed _____

III. Translate the following sentences into Chinese.

1. The press working process is to apply the large forces by press tools for a short time interval in order to produce the shearing or deformation of the work material.

2. The cushion is the press accessory located beneath or within a bolster for producing an upward motion and force; it is actuated by air, oil, rubber, or springs or a combination of mechanisms.

3. The blank holder contacts the stamping at about the time when the draw slide is halfway down on its stroke.

IV. Choose the correct answer for each sentence according to the text.

1. The press working process is widely used for the production of a _____.
   A. single part   B. few parts   C. middle batch   D. large number

2. In a mechanical press, the flywheel is used to _____.
   A. speed up the rotating speed of the electric motor
   B. release energy to the slide
   C. absorb the deformation energy of the material
   D. reduce the deflection of the press
3. "Double-action presses" means that _____.
   A. the press has two slides   B. the press can be mounted with two dies
   C. the press works twines one stroke   D. the press has a double force
4. In a double-action press, the draw slide is _____.
   A. mounted on the uprights   B. mounted on the gibs
   C. sliding within the blank holder slide D. sliding within the plunger
5. Compared with other forging machines, the hydraulic press is good because_____.
   A. it eliminates the heat transfer from workpiece to die
   B. the working speed is higher than other machines
   C. the investment is less to purchase a new machine for the same use
   D. the pressure can be changed as desired at any point in the stroke by adjusting the pressure control valve

Task 2.2　Injection-molding Machines

The greatest plastic parts are made by injection molding. The process consists of feeding a plastic compound in powdered or granular form from a hopper through metering and melting stages, and then injecting it into a mold.[1] After a brief cooling period, the mold is opened and the solidified part ejected. The major components of a common injection molding machine are as shown in Fig. 2.2.

injection mold 注射模

granular 粒状的
hopper 料斗
metering 计量，测定

clamping end 合模端

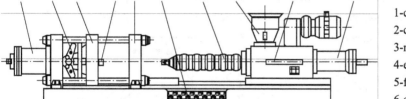

Fig. 2.2　The injection-molding machine

1-clamping hydraulic cylinder;
2-clamping mechanism;
3-moving plate;
4-ejector rod;
5-fixed plate;
6-control panel;
7-cylinder and heater;
8-hopper;
9-metering and feeding control;
10-injection hydraulic cylinder

The single-stage reciprocating screw system (Fig. 2.3)has become more popular because it prepares the material more thoroughly for the mold and is faster. The screw acts as a combination injection and plasticizing unit. As the plastic is fed to the rotating screw, it passes through three zones: feed, compression, and metering. After the feed zone, the screw-flight depth is gradually reduced, forcing the plastic to compress. The work converted to heat by shearing the plastic makes it a semifluid mass. In the metering zone, additional heat is applied by conduction from the barrel surface. As the chamber in front of the screw becomes filled, it forces the screw back, tripping a limit switch that activates a hydraulic cylinder that forces the screw forward and injects the fluid plastic into the closed mold.[2] An antiflow- back valve prevents plastic under pressure from escaping back into the screw flights.

injection end 注射端
ejector rod 顶杆
control panel 控制台
reciprocate 往复移动
screw 螺杆，螺钉
feed 进给
screw-flight 螺纹
work 功
semifluid 半流质的
barrel 料筒
chamber 室，膛
trip 松开，切断
activate 开动，触发

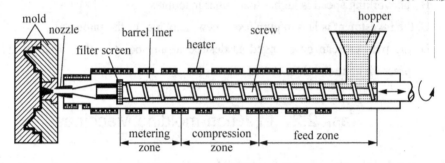

Fig. 2.3　The reciprocating screw injection system

The oldest way of injection molding is the single plunger method, sketched in Fig.2.4. When the plunger is drawn back, raw material falls from hopper into the chamber. The plunger is driven forward to force the material through the heating cylinder where it is soften and squirted under pressure into the mold. In a two-stage system (Fig.2.5), the material is plasticized in one cylinder, and a definite amount is transferred by a plunger or screw into a shot chamber from which a plunger injects the plastic into the mold.

nozzle 喷嘴
filter screen 过滤网
barrel liner 料筒衬套
plunger 柱塞，活塞
raw 未加工的
squirt 喷出
sprue 浇口
spreader 分流锥

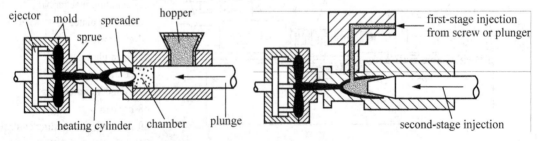

Fig. 2.4　Conventional single-stage plunger　　Fig. 2.5　two-stage injection molding system

An injection molding machine heats to soften, molds, and cools to harden a thermoplastic material. Operating-temperature is generally between 150~380℃ with full pressure usually over 35 and up to 350 MPa. The mold is water cooled in order to remove the pieces without distortion. The molded pieces and sprue are withdrawn from the injection side and ejected from the other side when the mold is open. The mold is then closed and clamped to start another cycle. Many reciprocating-screw machines are able to handle thermosetting plastic materials. Previously these materials were handled by compression or transfer molding. Thermosetting materials polymerized in the mold and are ejected hot in the range of 190~210℃. Thus thermosetting cycles can be faster. Of course the mold must be heated rather than chilled as with thermoplastics.

clamp 夹紧，夹住
handle 处理，操作
compression mold 压缩模，压制模
transfer mold 传递模，压注模
chill 冷却，变冷
sandwich 夹心，夹层

Machines are available for molding sandwich parts. One cylinder injects a measured amount of skin material into the die, and then a second cylinder squirts the filler inside the mass. Finally, a final spurt from the first cylinder clears the core material from the sprue. The aim is to produce composites with optimum properties. Either case or core may be foamed.

composite 合成物
core 中心，核心

Notes

1. The process consists of feeding a plastic in powdered or granular form from a hopper through metering and melting stages and then injecting it into a mold.

(注射)过程是：首先经过计量和熔化阶段从给料斗进给粉末状或粒状的塑料混合物，然后再将其注射到模具中。

2. As the chamber in front of the screw becomes filled, it forces the screw back, tripping a limit switch that activates a hydraulic cylinder that forces the screw forward and injects the fluid plastic into the closed mold.

当螺杆前方的空腔被塑料填满时，会迫使螺杆向后退，断开限位开关，从而启动液压缸，进而液压缸驱动螺杆向前运动，将液态塑料注射到闭合的模具中。

that activates a hydraulic… into the closed mold 是修饰 a limit switch 的限制性定语从句，其中的 that forces the screw…into the closed mold 是修饰 a hydraulic cylinder 的限制性定语从句。

New Words and Expressions

injection mold 注射模
compression mold 压缩模，压制模

nozzle ['nɔzl] n. 管口，喷嘴
antiflowback valve 防止倒流的阀，反流阀

transfer mold 传递模，压注模
powdered ['paudəd] adj. 粉末状的
granular ['grænjulə] adj. 粒状的
metering ['miːtəriŋ] n. 计量，测量
clamp [klæmp] v. 夹紧，钳住 n. 钳子，夹具
rod [rɔd] n. 杆，棒
panel ['pænl] n. 面板，仪表板；座谈小组
reciprocate [ri'siprəkeit] v. 往复运动；互换
screw [skruː] n. 螺纹，螺杆 v. 旋，拧
convert [kən'vəːt] v. 使……转变，转换
semifluid [,semi'fluːid] n. & adj. 半流质(的)
barrel ['bærəl] n. 桶 v. 装入桶内
chamber ['tʃeimbə] n. 室，腔，房间
trip [trip] v. 松开，断开；旅行
switch [switʃ] n. 开关，电闸 v. 转换，转变
activate ['æktiveit] v. 刺激，开动，激化

escape [is'keip] v. 逃脱，溜走
plunger ['plʌndʒə] n. 活塞，柱塞
raw [rɔː] adj. 未加工的
squirt [skwəːt] v. 喷出
sprue [spruː] n. 浇口，注入口
spreader ['spredə] n. 分流锥；推广者
withdraw [wið'drɔː] v. 撤退，收回，移开
handle ['hændl] v. 处理，操作
filler ['filə] n. 填充物；活页纸；漏斗
liner ['lainə] n. 衬垫；班机；划线者
spurt [spəːt] n. & v. 喷射，冲刺
chill [tʃil] v. 冷却，变冷
sandwich ['sænwidʒ] n. 夹心，夹层
composite ['kɔmpəzit] n. 合成物 adj. 合成的
core [kɔː] n. 果核，中心，核心
foam [fəum] n. 泡沫 v. 使起泡沫

Exercises

I. Complete the following sentences according to the text.

1. The injection molding consists of _____ a plastic compound in powdered or granular form from a _____ through _____ and melting stages, and then _____ it into a mold.

2. As the plastic is fed to the rotating _____, it passes through three zones: _____, _____, and _____. After the feed zone, the screw-flight _____ is gradually _____, forcing the plastic to _____.

3. The thermoplastic mold is water _____ in order to remove the pieces without _____. The molded pieces and _____ are withdrawn from the _____ side and _____ from the other side when the mold is _____.

4. Many _____-screw machines are able to _____ thermosetting plastic materials. Previously these materials were handled by _____ or _____ molding.

5. Machines are available for molding _____ parts, whose case or _____ may be foamed.

II. Translate the following phrases into Chinese or English.

1. 注射模 _____ 2. 压缩模 _____ 3. 传递模 _____
4. 定量区 _____ 5. 限位开关 _____ 6. 起泡沫 _____
7. hopper _____ 8. sprue _____ 9. barrel _____ 10. plunger _____
11. a reciprocating-screw machine _____ 12. clamping end _____

III. Read the following passage and answer the question.

The clamping force that a machine is capable of exerting is part of the size designation and is measured in tons. A rule-of-thumb can be used to determine the tonnage required for a particular job. It is based on two tons of clamp force per square inch of projected area. If the flow pattern is difficult and the parts are thin, this may have to go to three or four tons.

New Words

rule-of-thumb 概测法，粗略的计算方法　project 射出，发射　pattern 图案，样式，格调

Question: How does one go about determining the required clamping force for a particular mold?

Project 3

Press Forming Processes and Dies

Task 3.1 Forging

Forging is , as far as we know, the oldest metalworking process. In the early dawn of civilization mankind discovered that a heated piece of metal was more easily hammered into different shapes.[1] Forging can be defined as the working of a piece of metal into a desired shape by hammering or, pressing usually after it has been heated to improve its plasticity. The forgings' sizes range from less than 0.5 kg to over 200 tons. Usually steam, air or helve hammers, or hydraulic presses are used. In most cases, the metal to be forged is heated to its correct forging temperature, but sometimes cold- forging is done. Cold-forging is done in the range from room temperature up to the critical temperature of the metal.

forging 锻造
dawn 开始，黎明
civilization 文明
hammer 锤子，锤打
helve 柄，把手

The metal may be worked by three general forging operations: drawing out, upsetting, and squeezing. The forging processes can be grouped under four principal methods as: smith forging, drop forging, press forging, and upset forging.

Forgings are generally superior in mechanical properties to castings with the same chemical analysis for at least three reasons. First, the fiber flow lines when properly controlled and directed tend to provide higher strengths. Second, the forging process produces a dense structure usually free from voids, blowholes, or porosity. Third, the forging process helps to refine the grain size of the metal. The working of the metal breaks up coarse grains by producing a slip along crystallographic planes. Therefore, parts which must withstand

drawing out 拉拔
upset 镦粗
squeeze 冲压，压榨
smith forging 手工锻造
drop forging 落锤锻造
press forging 压锻
upset forging 镦粗
superior 优胜的
analysis 分析
dense 致密的
void 气孔，沙眼

severe stresses are preferably made by forging.

The tools necessary to produce a given forging cannot be made until the shape of the final forging has been determined.[2] Therefore, it is essential that the tool designer has an understanding of the underlying principles of forging design. These will be considered in the following order: forging draft, parting planes, fillets and corner radii, shrinkage and die wear, mismatch of dies, tolerances, and finish allowances.

When selecting the parting line on forgings, consideration must be given to the flow of metal and the directions of the resulting fiber low lines. A flat parting surface in a single horizontal plane should be selected if possible, because irregular parting surfaces may create a side thrust and they add to the cost of the dies. The standard draft angle is 7° since smaller draft angles cause more rapid die wear and increase the likelihood of the forgings sticking in the die. Interior surfaces require more draft, usually 10°, since the forgings will shrink around those portions of the die as they cool if several blows are to be struck.

No-draft forgings are used most often on nonferrous alloys. They are usually mounted in a die set and run in a forging press. Depending on the shape of the part, two or more sides of the die cavity are movable to allow the most conventional forgings and the production rates are much slower. In many cases, the parts are run once with the die not completely closed, excess flash material is removed and then the part is reheated and run a second time with the die closed completely.

Forging dies must withstand severe strains, resist wear, keep cracking and checking at a minimum, and have a long life under high-production conditions.[3] In order to obtain these properties, Cr-Ni-Mo, Cr-Ni, or Cr-Mo alloy steels are used as die materials.

blowhole 气孔
porosity 孔隙，松孔
slip 滑动
stress 应力
crystallographic 晶体的
withstand 抵抗
fillet 倒角

horizontal 水平的

stick 粘住
shrink 收缩
blow 通气孔

mount 安放

excess 多余的
flash 毛刺

severe 严重的，严厉的
strain 应变
checking 裂纹

Notes

1. In the early dawn of civilization mankind discovered that a heated piece of metal was more easily hammered into different shapes.

在人类文明初期，就发现加热过的金属更容易被锤打成各种不同的形状。

that a heated…different shapes 是谓语动词 discovered 的宾语从句。

2. The tools necessary to produce a given forging cannot be made until the shape of the final forging has been determined.

只有当锻件的最后形状确定后，生产给定锻件所需的工具才能制作出来。

3. Forging dies must withstand severe strains, resist wear, keep cracking and checking at a minimum, and have a long life under high-production conditions.

锻造用的模具必须能够承受严重的应变和应力，抵抗磨损，将裂纹抑制到最小程度，而且在大量生产的条件下有较长的寿命。

此句中的 withstand、resist、keep、have 是 4 个并列关系的谓语。

New Words and Expressions

forging [ˈfɔːdʒɪŋ] *n.* 锻造；锻件
dawn [dɔːn] *n.* 开始；黎明
civilization [sivəliˈzeiʃən] *n.* 文明，文化
hammer [ˈhæmə] *n.* 锤子 *v.* 锤打
helve [helv] *n.* 柄，把手 *v.* 给……装柄
upsetting [ʌpˈsetɪŋ] *n.* 镦(粗)；倾复，倒转
superior [sjuːˈpɪərɪə] *adj.* 高级的，优胜的
analysis [əˈnælɪsɪs] *n.* 分析，分解
dense [dens] *adj.* 稠密的，浓密的
void [vɔɪd] *n.* 孔穴，砂眼，气孔，蜂窝
blowhole [ˈbləʊhəʊl] *n.* 铸孔，气泡
porosity [pɔːˈrɒsɪti] *n.* 孔隙，(密集)气孔
withstand [wɪðˈstænd] *v.* 抵挡，经受住
coarse [kɔːs] *adj.* 粗糙的，粗鄙的
slip [slɪp] *n. & v.* 滑动，滑倒
crystallographic [krɪstəˈlɒɡræfɪk] *adj.* 晶体的
essential [ɪˈsenʃəl] *adj.* 必需的，基本的

underlying [ˌʌndəˈlaɪɪŋ] *adj.* 根本的，潜在的
principle [ˈprɪnsəpl] *n.* 原理，法则
draft [drɑːft] *n.* 拔模斜度；草稿，草图
fillet [ˈfɪlɪt] *n. & v.* 倒角
radius [ˈreɪdjəs] *n.* 半径(*pl.* radii [ˈreɪdiaɪ])
shrinkage [ˈʃrɪŋkɪdʒ] *n.* 收缩
tolerance [ˈtɒlərəns] *n.* 公差；容忍
horizontal [ˌhɒrɪˈzɒntl] *adj.* 地平线的，水平的
thrust [θrʌst] *n.* 推(拉)力，侧向压力
likelihood [ˈlaɪklɪhʊd] *n.* 可能性
stick [stɪk] *v.* 粘住，粘贴；刺，戳
flash [flæʃ] *n.* 毛刺
blow [bləʊ] *n.* 吹气，通气孔(管)
strike [straɪk] *v.* 铸造(*p.p.* struck)
mount [maʊnt] *v.* 安放，设置，装上；爬上
checking [ˈtʃekɪŋ] *n.* 裂纹，微裂；检查

Exercises

I. Answer the following questions according to the text.

1. What determines whether hot or cold forging is to be done?
2. What is forging draft?
3. What are the four types of forging processes?
4. What are the superior mechanical properties of forging?

II. Translate the following phrases into Chinese or English.

1. 拔模斜度 _____
2. 分型面 _____
3. 镦　粗 _____
4. 收 缩 量 _____
5. 拉　拔 _____
6. 临界温度 _____
7. 加工余量 _____
8. 晶　面 _____
9. smith forging _____
10. side thrust _____
11. 模具型腔 _____
12. 抑制裂纹 _____

Task 3.2 Blanking Principles

In the following discussion, certain die terms will be used frequently, Fig.3.1 presents the terms most commonly encountered.

term 术语
encounter 遇到，遭遇

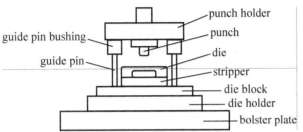

Fig. 3.1 Common components of a simple die

The cutting of metal between die components is a shearing process (Fig.3.2) in which the metal is stressed in shear between two cutting edges to the point of fracture, or beyond its ultimate strength.[1] The metal is subjected to both tensile and compressive stresses. Stretching beyond the elastic limit occurs, then plastic deformation, reduction in area, and finally, fracturing starts through cleavage planes in the reduced area and becomes complete.

compressive 压缩的
tensile 拉伸的
shearing 剪切
fracture 断裂
ultimate strength 极限应力
elastic limit 弹性极限
cleavage 分裂，劈裂

Fig. 3.2 Stresses in die cutting

The pressure applied by the punch on the metal tends to deform it into the die opening. When the elastic limit is exceeded by further loading, a part of the metal will be forced into the die opening in the form of an embossed pad on the lower face of the material. A corresponding depression results on the upper face. As the load is further increased, the punch will penetrate the metal to a certain depth and force an equal portion of metal thickness into the die. This penetration occurs before fracturing starts and reduces the cross-sectional area of metal through which the cut is being made. Fracture will start in the reduced area at both upper

punch 冲头
exceed 超越，超过

embossed 凸出的
pad 垫子
corresponding 相应的
penetrate 渗透，刺入

and lower cutting edges. If the clearance is suitable for the material being cut, these fractures will spread toward each other and finally meet, causing complete separation.² Further travel of the punch will carry the cut portion through the stock and into the die opening. (Fig.3.3)

cutting edge 刃口，剪切刃

stock 原料
die opening 模具内腔

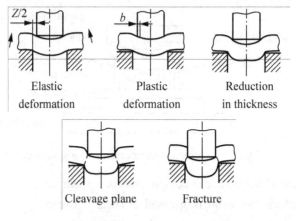

Fig. 3.3 Steps in shearing metal

If the contour to be blanked is irregular shaped, the sum of shearing forces on the two sides of the center of the ram may greatly not equal. Such irregularity results in a bending moment in the press ram, and undesirable deflections and misalignment. It is therefore necessary to find a point about which the sum of the shearing forces are symmetrical. This point is called the center of pressure, and is the center of gravity of the perameter of the blank edge. It is not the center of gravity of area. The press tool will be designed so so that the center of pressure will be on the axis of the press ram when the tool is mounted in the press.

contour 轮廓

bending moment 弯矩
deflection 偏转，偏斜
misalignment 偏心
symmetrical 对称的
center of pressure 压力中心

mount 安放，装配

Clearence is the space between the mating menbers of a die set. Proper clearance between cutting edges enable the fractures to meet. The fracture portion of the sheared edge will have a clean appearance with proper clearance. For optimum finish of a cut edge(Fig.3.4), proper clearance is necessary and is a function of the type, thickness, and temper of the work material. The upper corner of the cut edge of the stock and the lower corner of the blank will have a radius where the punch and die edges, respectively, make contact with the material. This radiusing is due to the plastic deformation taking place, and will be more pronounced when cutting soft metals.³ Excessive clearance will cause a large radius at these corners, as well as a burr on opposite corners.

clearance 间隙
mating 配合，啮合
optimum 最好的

temper 性质

respectively 分别地

pronounced 明显的
excessive 过多的
burr 毛刺，毛口
opposite 对面的

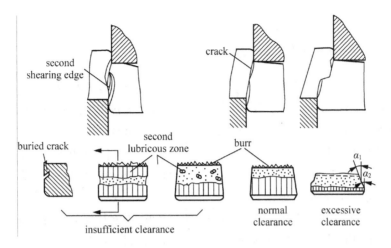

Fig. 3.4 Cut-edge characteristics of die-cut metal

Press tonnage is a total of forces requied to cut and form the part with a 30% safety factor added. In many cases, you will have to add stripping force if stripping is being done with a spring-loaded stripper, because the press has to compress the springs while cutting the material. Likewise, any spring pressure for forming, draw pads, and the like, will have to be added.

tonnage 吨位
safety factor 安全因子
strip 卸料
spring 弹簧，弹性

Notes

1. The cutting of metal between die components is a shearing process in which the metal is stressed in shear between two cutting edges to the point of fracture, or beyond its ultimate strength.

利用凹凸模切割金属是一个剪切过程，在这个过程中，位于两个刃口处的金属承受的剪切应力达到了断裂点，即超过了材料的极限应力。

in which the metal is stressed…ultimate strength 是 shearing process 的定语从句。

die components 直译为"模具组件，模具零件"，这里意译为"凹凸模"。

2. If the clearance is suitable for the material being cut, these fractures will spread toward each other and eventually meet, causing complete separation.

如果(凹凸模)间隙适于所需冲裁的材料，这些断口将相互扩展直至最终相遇，从而引起材料完全分离。

spread 和 meet 是两个递进关系的谓语动词，共用主语 these fracture, causing complete separation 是结果状语从句。

3. This radiusing is due to the plastic deformation taking place, and will be more pronounced when cutting soft metals.

这个圆角半径是由于材料发生塑性变形引起的，并且在冲裁比较软的金属材料时圆角半径会更大。

the plastic deformation taking place 是独立主格动名词作 be due to 的宾语。

New Words and Expressions

term [tə:m] *n.* 术语
encounter [in'kauntə] *n. & v.* 遇到，遭遇
compressive [kəm'presiv] *adj.* 压缩的,有压力的
tensile ['tensail] *adj.* 拉伸的
shearing ['ʃiəriŋ] *n.* 剪切
fracture ['fræktʃə] *n.* 断裂，破裂，骨折
ultimate strength ['ʌltimit streŋθ] 极限应力
elastic limit [i'læstik 'limit] 弹性极限
cleavage ['kli:vidʒ] *n.* 分裂，劈裂
punch [pʌntʃ] *n.* 冲头
exceed [ik'si:d] *v.* 超越，超过
embossed [im'bɔst] *adj.* 凸出的，浮雕的
pad [pæd] *n.* 垫子
corresponding [ˌkɔris'pɔndiŋ] *adj.* 相应的
penetrate ['penitreit] *v.* 渗透，刺入，看穿
cutting edge 刃口，剪切刃
stock [stɔk] *n.* 原料，库存，股票，树干
die opening 模具内腔，凹模型腔
contour ['kɔntuə] *n.* 轮廓，外形

bending moment 弯矩
deflection [diflekʃən] *n.* 偏转，偏斜
misalignment [tə:m] *n.* 偏心，轴线不重合
symmetrical [si'metrikəl] *adj.* 对称的,均匀的
mount [maunt] *n. & v.* 安放，装配
clearance ['kliərəns] *n.* 间隙，清理，缺口
mating ['meitiŋ] *n.* 配合，啮合
optimum ['ɔptiməm] *adj.* 最好的，最适宜的
temper ['tempə] *n.* 性质，脾气，回火
respectively [ri'spektivli] *adv.* 分别地，各个的
pronounced [prə'naunst] *adj.* 明显的
excessive [ik'sesiv] *adj.* 过多的，过分的
burr [bə:] *n.* 毛刺，毛口
opposite ['ɔpəzit] *adj.* 对面的，相对的
tonnage ['tʌnidʒ] *n.* 吨位
factor ['fæktə] *n.* 因子，因素，系数
strip [strip] *n. & v.* 卸料
spring [spriŋ] *n.* 弹簧，弹性
be subjected to 发生，遭受，服从

Exercises

I. Answer the following questions according to the text.

1. What is the center of pressure? When the contour to be blanked is irregularly shaped? Why must the center of pressure be calculated?

2. Describe shear action in die cutting operations.

3. What is the fundamental steps in shearing or cutting?

4. Why is necessary for proper clearance in shearing?

II. Translate the following phrases into Chinese or English.

1. 冲　裁_____　　2. 刃　口_____　　3. 塑性变形_____　　4. 间　隙_____
5. 拉　拔_____　　6. 安全因子_____　　7. 弹簧加载卸料板_____

Task 3.3 Piercing and Blanking Die

Piercing Die

Any complete press tool, consisting of a combination of mating members for producing pressworked parts, including all supporting and actuating elements. Pressworked terminology commonly defines the female part of any complete press tool as a die (Fig.3.5, Fig3.6).

actuate 驱动，促使
terminology 术语
pillar/post 柱

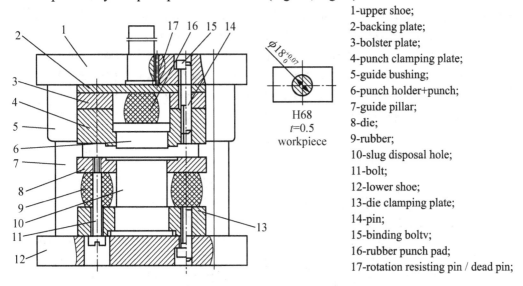

1-upper shoe;
2-backing plate;
3-bolster plate;
4-punch clamping plate;
5-guide bushing;
6-punch holder+punch;
7-guide pillar;
8-die;
9-rubber;
10-slug disposal hole;
11-bolt;
12-lower shoe;
13-die clamping plate;
14-pin;
15-binding boltv;
16-rubber punch pad;
17-rotation resisting pin / dead pin;

Fig. 3.5 Typical single-station piercing die

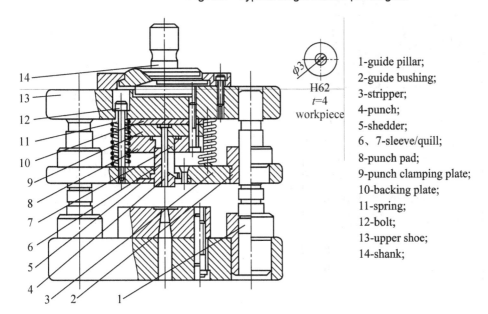

1-guide pillar;
2-guide bushing;
3-stripper;
4-punch;
5-shedder;
6、7-sleeve/quill;
8-punch pad;
9-punch clamping plate;
10-backing plate;
11-spring;
12-bolt;
13-upper shoe;
14-shank;

Fig. 3.6 Another single-station piercing die

The guide pins, pillars, or posts, are mounted in the lower shoe. The upper shoe contains bushings which slide on the guide pins. The assembly of of the lower and upper shoes with guide pins and bushings is a die set. Die sets in many sizes and designs are commercially available.

assembly 装配，集合
commercially 商业地
available 可利用的
sleeve/quill 衬套

A punch holder mounted to the upper shoe holds the punch. Sometimes a sleeve, or quill encloses the small punch to prevent its buckling under the ram pressure. The punch in a piercing die holes the diameter required.

Since the stock or workpiece can cling to a punch on the upstroke, it may be necessary to strip the material from the punch. Spring-loaded tripper holds the work material against the die block until the punch is withdrawn from the punched holes. A workpiece to be pierced is commonly held and located in a nest composed of flat plates shaped to encircle the outside part contours. Stock is positioned in dies by pins, block, or other locating stops for before the downstroke of the ram.

cling 附着，粘紧
upstroke 上行程

downstroke 下行程
nest 槽，巢
stock 原料
position 定位

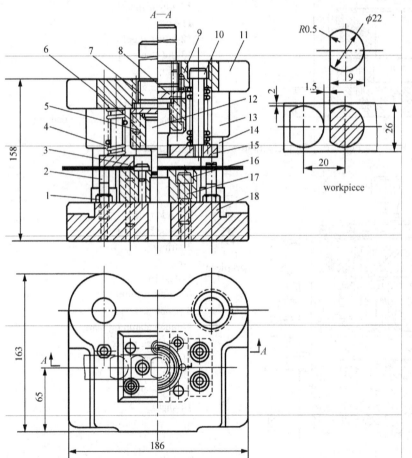

1、16-binding bolt;
2-locating pin;
3-stock guide pin;
4-spring;
5-pin;
6-punch clamping plate;
7-shank;
8-backing plate;
9-quill;
10-stripper bolt;
11-upper shoe;
12-punch;
13-guide bushing;
14-guide pillar;
15-stripper;
17-die;
18-lower shoe;

Fig. 3.7 A single-station blanking die

A compound die performs only cutting operations (usually blanking and piercing) which are completed during a single press stroke. A compound die can produce pierced blanked to close flatness and dimensional tolerances. A characteristic of compound dies is the inverted position of the blanking punch and blanking die. As shown in Fig. 3.8, the blanking die is fastened to the upper shoe and the blanking punch is mounted on the lower shoe. The blanking punch also functions as the piercing die, having a tapered hole in it and in the lower show for slug disposal.

blanking 冲裁, 落料
piercing 冲孔
inverted 倒置的
tapered 锥形的
slug 落料
disposal 处理, 清理

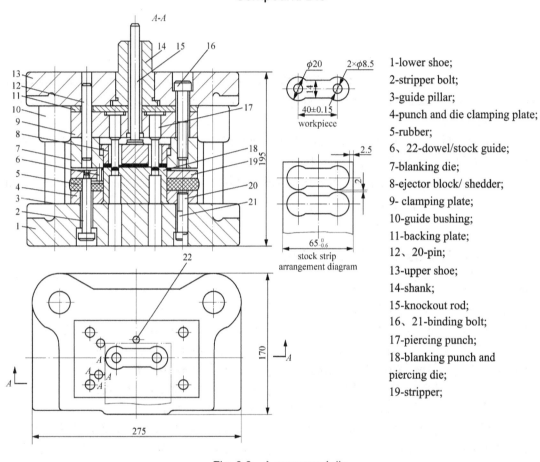

1-lower shoe;
2-stripper bolt;
3-guide pillar;
4-punch and die clamping plate;
5-rubber;
6、22-dowel/stock guide;
7-blanking die;
8-ejector block/ shedder;
9- clamping plate;
10-guide bushing;
11-backing plate;
12、20-pin;
13-upper shoe;
14-shank;
15-knockout rod;
16、21-binding bolt;
17-piercing punch;
18-blanking punch and piercing die;
19-stripper;

Fig. 3.8 A compound die

On the upstroke of the press slide, the knockout bar of the press strikes the knockout collar, forcing the knockout rod and shedder downward, thus pushing the finished workpiece out of the blanking die.[1] The stock strip is guided by stock guides screwed to the stripper. On the upstroke the stock is stripped from the blanking punch by the upward travel of the stripper. Before the cutting cycle starts, the strip stock is held flat between the stripper and the bottom surface of the blanking die.

collar 圈
shedder 卸料块

Four special shoulder stripper bolts, commercially available, guide the stripper in its travel and retain it against the preload of rubber or springs.

retain 留住，保持

The blanking die and clamping plate is screwed and doweled to the upper shoe.

A spring-loaded shedder pin (oil-seal breaker) incorporated in the shedder is depressed when the shedder pushes the blanked part from the die. On this upstroke of the ram the shedder pin breaks the oil seal between the surfaces of the blanked part and shedder, allowing the part to fall out of the blanking die.

oil-seal breaker 油封断路器

Notes

1. On the upstroke of the press slide, the knockout bar of the press strikes the knockout collar, forcing the knockout rod and shedder downward, thus pushing the finished workpiece out of the blanking die.

在压力机滑块的上行程中，压力机的打料杆碰到打料环，从而施力给打料杆和卸料块下移，从而将成品件从落料凹模中推出。

forcing the knockout rod and shedder downward 和 pushing the finished workpiece out of the blanking die 为现在分词短语作结果状语。

New Words and Expressions

actuate ['æktjueit] v. 驱动，促使
terminology [ˌtəːmiˈnɔlədʒi] n 术语
pillar/post ['pilə/pəust] n 柱
assembly [əˈsembli] n 装配，集合
commercially [kəˈməːʃəli] adv. 商业地
available [əˈveiləbl] adj.可利用的，可用到的
sleeve [sliːv] n. 套(筒，管)，衬套；空心轴
quill [kwil] n. 套筒轴，主轴，钻轴，滚针
cling [kliŋ] v. 附着，粘紧
upstroke [ˈʌpstrəuk] n. 上行程
downstroke [ˈdaunˌstrəuk] n. 下行程
nest [nest] n. 槽，巢

stock [stɔk] n. 原料，库存，股票，树干
position [pəˈziʃən] n. & v. 定位
blanking [ˈblæŋkiŋ] n. 冲裁，落料
piercing [ˈpiəsiŋ] n. 冲孔，刺穿
inverted [inˈvəːtid] adj. 倒置的
tapered [ˈteipəd] adj. 锥形的
slug [slʌg] n. 落料，嵌片
disposal [disˈpəuzəl] n. 处理，清理，安排
collar [ˈkɔlə] n. 圈，轴衬，法兰盘，衣领
shedder [ˈʃedə] n. 卸料块/装置/，推/拨/抛料机
retain [riˈtein] v. 留住，保持
oil-seal breaker 油封断路器

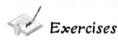 Exercises

I. Answer the following questions according to the text.

1. What is a die set?

2. What are the differences between piercing die and blanking die?
3. What are the major characteristics of compound dies?

II. Please write down the components' names in Fig. 3.9 in English.

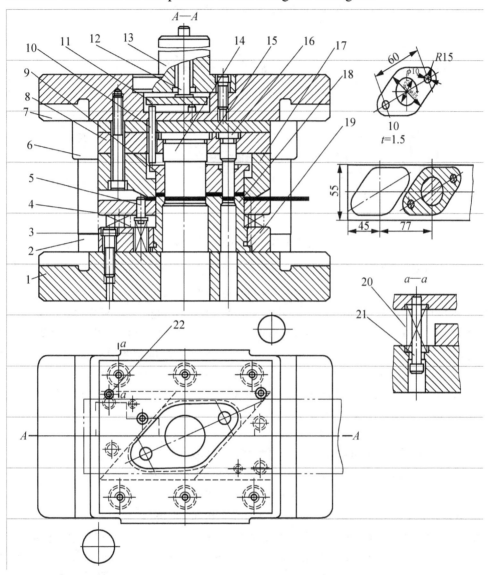

Fig. 3.9 A compound die

Task 3.4 Bending Die

Bending is the uniform straining of material, usually flat sheet or strip metal, around a straight axis which lies in the neutral plane and normal to the lengthways direction of the sheet or strip. The neutral axis is the plane area in bent metal where all strains are zero. Metal flow

straining 变形，应变
neutral plane 中性层
lengthways 纵向的
neutral axis 中性轴

takes place within the plastic range of the metal, so that the bend retains a permanent set after removal of the applied stress.[1] The inner surface of a bend is in compression, and the outer surface is in tension. A pure bending action does not reproduce the exact shape of the punch and die in the metal.

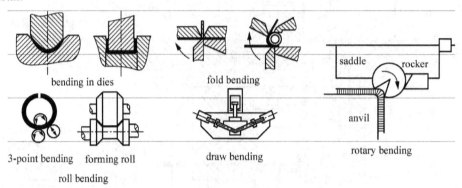

Fig.3.10 Methods of bending

Bend Radii(Fig.3.10): Minimum bend radii vary for different metals. Generally, different annealed metals can be bent to a radius equal to the thickness of the metal without cracking or weakening.

Bend Allowance(Fig.3.10): Since bent metal is longer after bending, its increased length may have to be considered by the die designer if the length tolerance of the bent part is critical. The length of bent metal may be calculated from the equation:

$$B = \frac{A}{360} 2\pi (R_i + Kt)$$

where B——bend allowance (mm); A——bend angle (°);
R_i——inside radius of bend (mm); t——metal thickness (mm);
$K = 0.33$ (when $R_i < 2t$) or $K = 0.50$ (when $R_i \geq 2t$)

bend radii 弯曲半径

cracking 开裂
weakening 强度降低
bent allowance 弯曲公差
critical 严格的
equation 方程，公式

V Bending(Fig.3.11): Metal sheet or strip, supported by a V block, is forced by a wedge-shaped punch into the die block. This method produces a bending having an included angle which may be acute, obtuse, or of 90°. Friction between a spring-loaded knurled pin in the V die and the part will prevent or reduce side creep of the part during its bending.[2]

Edge bending (Fig.3.11): It is cantilever loading of a beam. The bending punch 1 forces the metal against the supporting die 2.The bend axis is parallel to the edge of the die. The workpiece is clamped to the die block by a spring-loaded pad 3 before the punch contacts the workpiece to prevent its movement during downward travel of the punch.

wedge-shaped 楔形的
acute/obtuse 锐/钝角的
friction 摩擦
knurled pin 钩销
creep 微移，蠕动
cantilever 悬臂
beam 梁
parallel 平行的
spring-back 弹性回弹

Project 3 Press Forming Processes and Dies

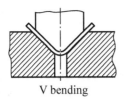 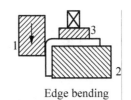

V bending　　　　　　　　Edge bending

Fig.3.11　V bending and Edge bending

Bending Force: For U bending (channel bending) pressures will be about twice those required for V bending; edge bending requires about 1/2 those needed for V bending.

Spring-back: After bending pressure on metal is released, the elastic stresses also are released, which causes metal movement resulting in a decrease in the bend angle as well as an increase in the included angle between the bent portions.[3] Such a metal movement, termed spring-back, varies in steel from 0.5~5°, depending upon its hardness, phosphor bronze may spring back from 10~15°.

V-bending dies customarily compensate for spring-back with V blocks and wedge-shaped punches having included angles somewhat less than that required in the part. The part is bent through a greater angle than that required but it spring back to the desired angle.

phosphor bronze 磷青铜
customarily 通常
compensate 补偿

Notes

1. Metal flow takes place within the plastic range of the metal, so that the bend retains a permanent set after removal of the applied stress.

金属的流动发生在金属的塑性变形范围内，因而当撤销所施加的外力后，金属的弯曲也会保留一个永久的形状。

2. Friction between a spring-loaded knurled pin in the V die and the part will prevent or reduce side creep of the part during its bending.

在 V 字形凹模内，弹簧加载钩销和零件间的摩擦会防止或减小零件在弯曲时的侧移。

pin 和 part 为介词短语 between…and…的两个介词宾语，其中，pin 前有两个过去分词 spring-loaded 和 knurled 作定语。

3. After bending pressure on metal is released, the elastic stresses also are released, which causes metal movement resulting in a decrease in the bend angle as well as an increase in the included angle between the bent partss.

当将作用在金属上的弯曲力去除后，弹性应力也随之消失，这样就引起了金属移动(弹性回弹)，导致弯曲角减小，即弯曲零件的包角增大。

which causes metal movement…between the bent parts 为其前面整个主句的非限制性定语从句，说明主句陈述的情况所产生的结果。

New Words and Expressions

straining [ˈstreiniŋ] n. 变形，应变
neutral [ˈnju:trəl] adj. 中性的，中立的
lengthways [ˈleŋθweiz] adj. & adv. 纵向的(地)
radii [ˈreidiai] n. 半径
cracking [ˈkrækiŋ] n. 开裂，破裂，裂化
weakening [ˈwi:kəniŋ] n. 强度降低，变弱
allowance [əˈlauəns] n. 公差，宽容
critical [ˈkritikəl] adj. 严格的，临界的
equation [iˈkweiʃən] n. 方程，等式，平衡
wedge-shaped [wedʒʃeipt] adj. 楔形的
acute [əˈkju:t] adj. 锐角的，尖锐的

obtuse [əbˈtju:s] adj. 钝角的，迟钝的
friction [ˈfrikʃən] n. 摩擦
knurled [ˈnə:ld] adj. 带钩的，有凸节的
creep [kri:p] v. 微移，蠕动
cantilever [ˈkæntili:və] n. 悬臂
beam [bi:m] n. 梁
parallel [ˈpærəlel] adj. 平行的
spring-back 弹性回弹
phosphor bronze [ˈfɔsfə brɔnz] 磷青铜
customarily [ˈkʌstəmərəli] adv. 通常
compensate [ˈkɔmpənseit] v. 补偿

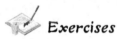 **Exercises**

I. Answer the following questions according to the text.

1. What is the basic principle involved in a bending die?
2. What causes spring-back?

II. Please remember the components' terms in Fig. 3.12.

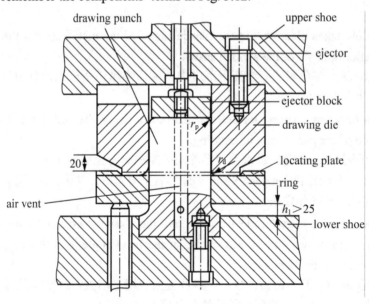

Fig. 3.12 The first step drawing die

Project 4

Plastic Forming Processes and Molds

Task 4.1 Injection Mold

The principle of injection molding is quite similar to that of die-casting. Plastic powder is loaded into the feed hopper and a certain amount feeds into the heating chamber when the plunger or screw draws back, where the plastic powder under heat and pressure becomes a fluid. After the mold is closed, the plunger or screw moves forward, forcing some of the fluid plastic into the mold cavity under pressures. Since the mold is cooled by circulating cold water, the plastic hardens and the part may be ejected when the plunger or screw draws back and the mold opens. The molds' internal surfaces are chromium-plated. Injection molding is principally used for the production of the thermoplastic parts, although some progress has been made in developing a method for thermosetting materials injection. The problem of injecting thermosetting plastics is that thermosetting plastics cure and harden under melted conditions within a few minutes.

The advantages of injection molding are:

(1) A high molding speed adapted for mass production is possible.

(2) There is a wide choice of thermoplastic materials providing a variety of useful properties.

---

injection mold 注射模
die-casting 压力铸造
hopper 料斗，漏斗
chamber 腔，室
plunger 柱塞

circulating 循环

chromium-plated 镀铬的
progress 改进，进步

(3) It is possible to mold threads, undercuts, side holes, and large thin sections.

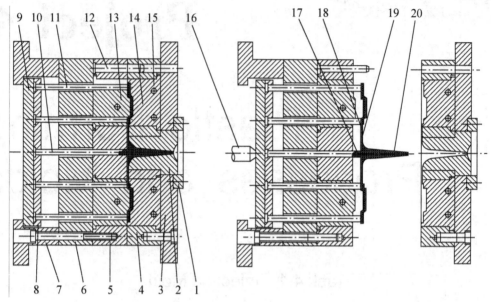

1-locating ring; 2-sprue bushing; 3-clamp plate; 4-cavity retainer plate; 5-core retainer plate; 6-support plate; 7-mold support; 8-ejector pin retainer plate; 9-ejector plate; 10-sprue puller pin; 11-ejector pin; 12-guide pillar; 13-core insert; 14-cavity insert; 15-waterway; 16-piston; 17-cold slug well; 18-gate; 19-runner; 20-sprue

Fig. 4.1 Conventional two-plate mold

New Words and Expressions

injection mold 注射模
die-casting 压力铸造
hopper [ˈhɔpə] n. 料斗，漏斗
chamber [ˈtʃeimbə] n. 腔，室
plunger [ˈplʌndʒə] n. 柱塞
circulating [ˈsəːkjuleitiŋ] adj. 循环，流通

chromium-plated [ˈkrəumjəm] adj. 镀铬的
progress [ˈprəugres] n. & v. 改进，进步
mass production 大量生产，大宗生产
thread [θred] n. 螺纹，线，思路
undercut [ˈʌndəkʌt] n. 铸件侧面凹进去的部分
side hole 侧孔

Exercises

Question: What are the advantages of injection molding ?

Task 4.2 Compression Mold

In compression molding the plastic material as powder or preforms is placed into a heated steel mold cavity (Fig.4.2). Since the parting surface is in a horizontal plane, the upper half of the mold descends vertically. It closes the mold cavity and applies heat and pressure for a predetermined period so that the plastic becomes a semiliquid which flows to all parts of the mold cavity. Usually 1 to 15 minutes is required for curing, although a recently developed alkyd plastic will cure in less than 25 seconds. The mold is then opened and the molded part removed. If metal inserts are desired in the parts, they should be placed in the mold cavity on pins or in holes before the plastic is loaded. Also, the preforms should be preheated before loading into the mold cavity to eliminate gases, improve flow, and decrease curing time. Dielectric heating is a convenient method of heating the preforms.

The thermosetting plastics which harden under heat and pressure are suitable for compression molding and transfer molding (Fig.4.3). It is not practical to mold thermoplastic materials by compression molding because the molds would have to be alternately heated and cooled, that is, the productive cycle is long. That gate and sprue are unnecessary results in a saving in material, because trimmed-off gate and sprue would be a complete loss of the. thermosetting plastic. The press used for compression molding is usually a vertical hydraulic press.

compression mold 压缩模
preform 预制件
parting surface 分型面
horizontal 水平的

alkyd 醇酸树脂
cure 固化，愈合

eliminate 排除，消除
dielectric 电介质，绝缘体

transfer mold 传递模

alternately 交替地

trimmed-off 被修掉的

vertical 立式的，垂直的

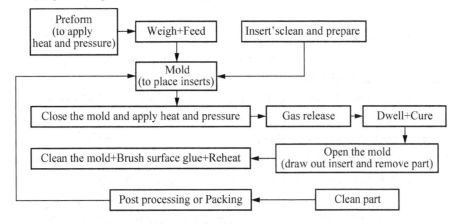

Fig. 4.2 Compression molding process

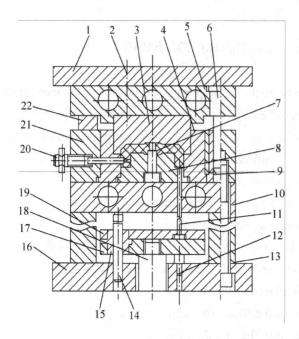

1-upper shoe; 2-bolt;
3- cavity; 4-core insert;
5、10-die clamping plate;
6-guide pin; 7-core insert;
8-core; 9-guide bushing;
11- ejector pin; 12-limit pin;
13-bolster; 14-ejector pillar;
15- ejector pillar bushing;
16-lower shoe; 17-ejector plate;
18-trail rod;
19-ejector pin retaining plate;
20-side insert;
21-die clamping plate;
22-backing plate ;

Fig. 4.3 Typical compression mold

 New Words and Expressions

compression mold 压缩模
preform [ˈpriːfɔːm] n. 预制件
parting surface 分型面
horizontal [ˌhɔriˈzɔntl] adj. 水平的
alkyd [ˈælkid] n. 醇酸树脂
cure [kjuə] v. 固化，愈合

eliminate [iˈlimineit] v. 排除，消除
dielectric [ˌdaiiˈlektrik] n. 电介质，绝缘体
transfer mold 传递模
alternately [ɔːlˈtəːnitli] adv. 交替地
trim [trim] v. 修整，修剪
vertical [ˈvəːtikəl] adj. 立式的，垂直的

Task 4.3 Major Parts Used for an Ejection System

A push back pin and a coil spring are used for regular molds (Fig. 4.4), whereas a push back pin and a gas spring are sometimes used for large size molds(Fig. 4.5).

1. Ejector Stopper (Stroke End Pin, as shown in Fig.4.6)
A block that stops an ejector plate from going forward.

2. Sprue Lock Pins (Sprue Puller)
A pin has the edge of which is undercut to pull a part in mold opening and remove a sprue from a sprue bush. After mold opening, this pin will function as an ejector pin and eject the sprue from a sprue bush. Also it releases gas contained in molten plastic.

coil spring 盘簧，圆弹簧
gas spring 气弹簧

推板制动销
ejector plate 推板
拉料杆
undercut 侧面有凹切口
sprue bush 浇口套
eject 推出
release 释放
contain 包含

Project 4 Plastic Forming Processes and Molds

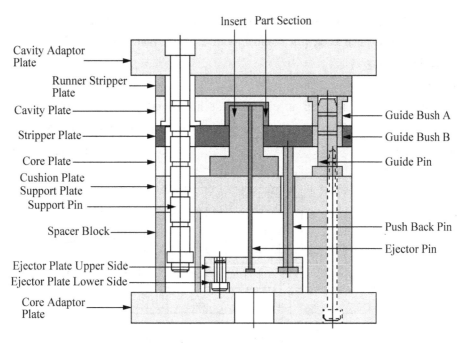

Fig. 4.4 An example of a regular mold

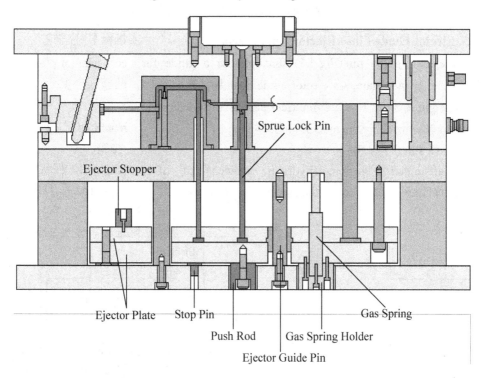

Fig. 4.5 An example of a large mold

3. Ejector Plate(Push Plate)   推板

A plate that supports an edge of an ejector pin or a push back pin to eject a part from a mold. It is ejected by an ejector

ejector/ push back pin
顶料杆，推料杆

device of a molding machine, and returned to the original position when the edge of a push back pin collides with a cavity plate during mold clamping.

4. Stop Pins

A stopper installed to keep an ejector plate horizontal or prevent the ejector plate from retreating too far and damaging a core adaptor plate.

original 初始的
collide 碰撞

止动销
stopper 阻塞物
horizontal 水平的
retreat 后退，撤退

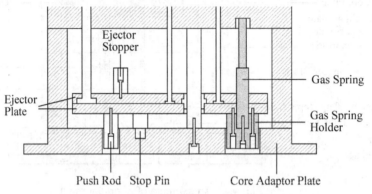

Fig. 4.6 Schematic of ejection system

5. Ejector Guide Pins / Ejector Guide Bush

An ejector guide pin (Fig.4.7) functions as a guide for sliding of an ejector plate. An ejector guide bush is also called a push plate guide bush. It is a cylindrical part used to determine the position by matching the ejector guide pin.

推板导柱/导套
core adaptor plate
凸模固定板

match 相配，匹配

6. Push Pin (Fig.4.8)

A shaft linked to the force (hydraulic or mechanical) of the molding machine in order to get the ejector plate to work.

推管
shaft 轴，杆状物
push rod 推/顶料杆

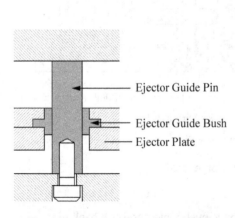

Fig. 4.7 Ejector guide pin and bush

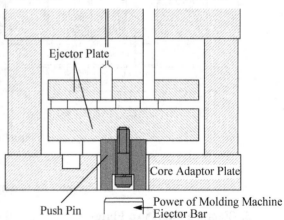

Fig. 4.8 Push pin

7. Gas Spring / Gas Spring Holder

A gas spring forcibly pushes back an ejector plate. The strength of the spring is adjusted by adjusting the filling pressure. When using a gas spring, make sure to avoid high temperature (heat may expand gas, deteriorating the original functions of a gas spring). A gas spring holder is a block used to fix a gas spring to an ejector plate. Counter bore process for a bolt installation hole, for it also functions as a push rod.

气弹簧/夹持器
forcibly 强制地，用力地
filling 供应
deteriorate 使恶化
counter 反向
bore 镗孔
bolt 螺栓
installation 安装

New Words and Expressions

coil [kɔil] n. & v. 卷，圈，盘卷
undercut [ˈʌndəkʌt] v. & adj. 侧面有凹切口
eject [iˈdʒekt] v. 逐出，撵出，驱逐，喷射
release [riˈliːs] v. 释放，解放，放弃，让与
contain [kənˈtein] v. 包含，容纳，容忍，自制
original [əˈridʒənəl] adj. 初始的，独创的
collide [kəˈlaid] v. 碰撞，抵触
stopper [ˈstɔpə] n. 阻塞物，塞子，制动器
horizontal [ˌhɔriˈzɔntl] adj. 水平的
retreat [riˈtriːt] n. & v. 后退，撤退

adaptor [əˈdæptə(r)] n. 插座，转接器
match [mætʃ] v. 相配，匹配 n. 火柴，比赛
shaft [ʃɑːft] n. 轴，杆状物
forcibly [ˈfɔːsəbli] adv. 强制地，用力地
filling [ˈfiliŋ] n. 填充，供应，注满
deteriorate [diˈtiəriəreit] v. 使恶化
counter [ˈkauntə] adj. 反向的 n. 计数器，柜台
bore [bɔː] v. 镗孔，钻孔，使烦扰
bolt [bəult] n. 螺栓，门闩
installation [ˌinstəˈleiʃən] n. 安装，安置，就职

Project 5

The Computers' Applications in Industry

Task 5.1 CAD/CAM

Since the advent of computer technology, manufacturing professionals have wanted to automate the design process and use the database developed therein for automating manufacturing processes. A key goal of CAD/CAM is to produce data can be used in manufacturing a product while developing the database for the design of that product (Fig.5.1). When the database is successfully implemented, CAD/CAM should remove the "wall" that has traditionally existed between the design and manufacturing components. CAD/CAM involves the sharing of a common database between the design and manufacturing components.[1]

Since the advent of CAD/CAM, other terms have developed:
(1) Computer-aided design and manufacturing (CAD/CAM)
(2) Computer-aided engineering (CAE)
(3) Computer graphics (CG)
(4) Computer-aided process planning (CAPP)
(5) Computer-aided design and drafting (CADD)

These spin-off terms all refer to specific aspects of the CAD/CAM concept. CAD/CAM itself is a broader, more inclusive term. It is at the heart of automated and integrated manufacturing.

advent 出现，到来
automate 使自动化
professional 专业人员
database 数据资料(库)

implement 贯彻，执行
traditionally 传统上

计算机辅助设计及制造
计算机辅助工程(分析)
计算机图形学
计算机辅助工艺设计
计算机辅助设计及绘图
spin-off 新兴的
inclusive 内容丰富的
integrated 集成的

Project 5　The Computers' Applications in Industry

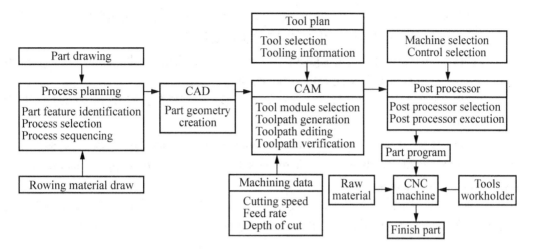

Fig. 5.1　The block diagram of a CAD/CAM system

Interactive computer graphics (ICG) plays an important role in CAD/CAM. Through the use of ICG, designers develop a graphic image of the product being designed while storing the data that electronically make up the graphic image.[2] The graphic image can be presented in a two-dimensional (2-D), three-dimensional (3-D), or solids format. ICG images are constructed using such basic geometric characters as points, lines, circles, and curves. Once created, these images can be easily edited and manipulated in a variety of ways including enlargements, reductions, rotations, and movements. An ICG system has three main components: ①hardware, which consists of the computer and various peripheral devices; ②software, which consists of the computer programs and technical manuals for the system (the popular ICG software used in CAD/CAM includes AutoCAD, UG, Pro/E, I-DEAS and CATIA etc.); ③the human designer, the most important of the three components.

interactive 交互式的
ICG 计算机图形交互

electronically 电子地

solids format 实体格式
geometric 几何的
manipulate 操作，处理
reduction 缩影，减少

peripheral 外围的
manual 手册，指南

The applications of CAD/CAM can continually improve a company's productivity, and, in turn, competitiveness. The rational for CAD/CAM are: increased productivity; better quality; better communication; common database with manufacturing; reduced prototype construction costs; faster response to customers.[3]

competitiveness 竞争
rational 合理之处，优点
prototype 样品，原型

 Notes

1. When the database is successfully implemented, CAD/CAM should remove the "wall" that has traditionally existed between the design and manufacturing components. CAD/CAM involves the sharing of a common database between the design and manufacturing components.

当数据库被成功创建时,传统上存在于零部件设计和制造之间的障碍就可以消除了。CAD/CAM 技术可以共享零部件设计和制造之间的通用数据资料。

2. Through the use of ICG, designer develop a graphic image of the product being designed while storing the data that electronically make up the graphic image.

通过使用计算机图形交互技术,在存储电子形式的图像数据时设计师可以绘制所要设计的产品图像。

3. The rational for CAD/CAM are: increased productivity; better quality; better communication; common database with manufacturing; reduced prototype construction costs; faster response to customers.

CAD/CAM 技术的优点在于:可提高生产率;获得的产品质量更好;通信更便捷;提供通用的产品制造数据资料;制作样品的费用减少;可以更快地响应客户要求。

New Words and Expressions

advent ['ædvənt] n. 出现,到来
automate ['ɔ:təmeit] v. 使自动化,自动化操作
professional [prə'feʃənl] n. 专业人员 adj. 专业的
database ['deitəbeis] n. 数据库
implement ['implimənt] v. 贯彻,执行 n. 工具
traditionally [trə'diʃənəl] adv. 传统上
spin-off 新兴的
inclusive [in'klu:siv] adj. 内容丰富的,包含的
integrated ['intigreitid] adj. 集成的

interactive [,intər'æktiv] adj. 交互式的 ICG 计算机图形交互
electronically [ilek'trɔnikəli] adv. 电子地
geometric [dʒiə'metrik] adj. 几何的
manipulate [mə'nipjuleit] v. 操作,处理
reduction [ri'dʌkʃən] n. 缩影,减少
peripheral [pə'rifərəl] adj. 外围的 n. 外围设备
manual ['mænjuəl] n. 手册,指南
competitiveness [kəm'petitivnis] n. 竞争
rational ['ræʃənl] n. 合理之处 adj. 合理的
prototype ['prəutətaip] n. 样品,原型

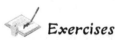
Exercises

I. Complete the following sentences according to the text.

1. The graphic image can be presented in a _____, _____, or _____.

2. An ICG system has three main components: _____, _____, and _____.

3. The applications of CAD/CAM can continually improve a company's _____, and, in turn, _____.

4. Once created, these images can be easily _____ and manipulated in a variety of ways including enlargements, _____, _____, and movements.

5. The rational for CAD/CAM are: increased _____; better _____; better communication; common _____ with manufacturing; reduced _____ construction costs; faster response to customers.

II. Translate the following phrases into English.

1. 计算机辅助设计与制造 _____ 2. 计算机辅助工程分析 _____
3. 计算机辅助工艺规划 _____ 4. 计算机辅助设计与绘图 _____
5. 计算机图形交互 _____ 6. 实体格式 _____ 7. 技术手册 _____

III. Translate the following sentences into Chinese.

1. Since the advent of computer technology, manufacturing professionals have wanted to automate the design process and use the database developed therein for automating manufacturing processes.

2. In the near future, some companies will not use drawings at all, but will be passing part information directly from design to manufacturing via a database.

Task 5.2 CAD/CAM's Applications

1. CAD's Benefits

The benefits of computer use in drafting and design tasks are impressive: increased speed, greater accuracy, reduction of hardcopy storage space as well as better recall, enhanced communication capabilities, improved quality and easier modification.

计算机辅助设计与绘图的优点

accuracy 精确性，准确性
recall 调用
enhance 增强
modification 更改，修正

2. Computer Aided Part Programming

Part programming software is used to ease programming for CNC machines when a complex part geometry requires calculation of a large number of tool positions. Part programming software is incorporated into a family of CAM software and has a dynamic graphics database to hold the actual machining sequences. These sequences can be viewed, edited, chained, or deleted.[1] The programming can be accomplished whether single cuts or CNC machine canned cycles will be used. The software will also automatically calculate the proper feeds and speeds to be used during the machining, create a tooling list, and define the tool path.

计算机辅助零件编程

ease 使……轻松，安逸
complex 复杂的

incorporate 合并，混合
dynamic 动态的，动力的
machining sequences 工序

tooling list 刀具列表
tool path 刀路

3. NC Cutter-Path Verification

Before a part is machined, the part program needs to be verified in order to eliminate potential errors during actual machining. There are several ways to verify a part program: to

数控刀具切削路径验证

verify 校验，核实

make a dry cut on the machine without the workpiece to detect gross programming mistakes; to actually machine a prototype in wax, plastic, wood, foam, or some other soft materials to verify only the geometry. When a part program is generated using a CAD/CAM system, a solid model may be used to generate a realistic picture of the workpiece, the cutter path and the finished part.[2] Real-time simulation of the cutting process can be displayed on screen. Most simulations are purely geometry-based, where the cutting condition is not considered.

4. Computer Aided Process Planning

Process planning, through which design information can be translated into manufacturing language, is the critical bridge between design and manufacturing.[3] Computer aided process planning has the following advantages: to reduce the requirement of skilled planners, time, and costs; to create more consistent and accurate plans; to increase productivity.

5. Group Technology

In a CAD system, the drawings are stored in a database. Group technology provides components with meaningful drawing numbers. Each drawing number is allocated by a coding system and each digit has meaning. If the code number is known, many of the component features can be deduced without reference to the drawing.

6. Materials Requirement Planning

Materials requirement planning have been available for some time, but with the advent of computers much more accurate information is available and the manufacturing system can respond to changes more easily. The bills of materials can come directly from the CAD system, which include the stock number, name of item, quantity in stock, unit of measure, minimum stock level, lead time of purchased or manufactured in-house, and the specifications of each component part and suppliers.[4]

7. Robotics

Industry robots are mechanical arms controlled by computer programs. Changing the program changes the set sequence of movements. Robots are widely used in automated assembly operations for circular and linear transfer.[5]

8. Computer Integrated Manufacturing

Computer integrated manufacturing is the term used to

---

eliminate 消除
potential 潜在的
dry cut 空切
detect 发觉
gross 粗略的
wax 石蜡
generate 产生
realistic 现实的
finished part 成品
simulation 仿真,模拟
计算机辅助工艺设计
critical 关键的,临界的

consistent 一致的,坚固的
accurate 精确的,正确的
成组技术

allocate 分配,分派
digit 数字

reference 参考
物料需求供给

bill 清单

lead time 提前时间
in-house 自制的
specification 规格
机械手(机器人)技术

assembly 装配
circular transfer line 盘式传送线
计算机集成制造

describe the most modern approach to manufacturing. CIM encompasses many of the other advanced manufacturing technologies such as CNC, CAD/CAM, robotics and just-in-time delivery. Integration means that a system can provide complete and instantaneous sharing of information.[6] In a CIM system, not only parts can be processed in computers and moved among machines automatically, but also the order of manufacturing operations can be sequenced automatically.

9. Flexible Manufacturing Systems

Both the assembly line and the transfer line (Fig.5.2) belong to the domain of fixed automation. Contrary to fixed automation, programmed automation is flexible and can handle large variety of part. The following figure clearly shows the recommended successful domain for each of the two automations. There exists a gap between the high-production transfer lines (fixed automation) and the low-production, though flexible, individual NC or CNC machines. This gap involves medium-roduction accompanied by a limited variety of part designs. The tailored products demanded by customers call for flexibility and medium-production. A reasonable solution is to develop a hybrid of fixed and programmed automation that combines the best features of both—appropriately called a flexible manufacturing system (FMS).

approach 方法，途径
encompass 包围，环绕
just-in-time delivery 即时交货

instantaneous 即时的

sequence 生成程序
柔性制造系统

domain 范围，领域
fixed automation 刚性自动化
flexible 灵活的

tailor 裁剪

hybrid 混合

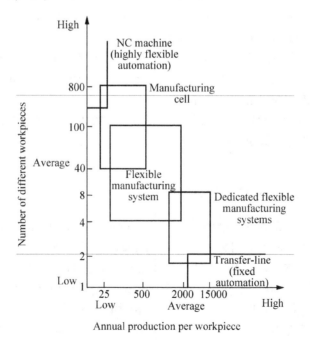

Fig. 5.2 Annual production per workpiece

Notes

1. Part programming software is incorporated into a family of CAM software and has a dynamic graphics database to hold the actual machining sequences. These sequences can be viewed, edited, chained, or deleted.

零件编程软件是 CAM 软件包中的一个软件，它有一个动态的图形数据库，可以支持实际的加工工序。这些加工工序可以被显示、编辑、串联或删除。

2. When a part program is generated using a CAD/CAM system, a solid model may be used to generate a realistic picture of the workpiece, the tools, the cutter path and the finished part.

当零件加工程序是使用 CAD/CAM 系统生成的时候，可以使用实体模型生成一幅工件、刀具、切削路径以及成品的逼真图片。

3. Process planning, through which design information can be translated into manufacturing language, is the critical bridge between design and manufacturing.

工艺设计是设计与制造之间的关键桥梁，设计信息只有通过工艺设计才能被转换成制造语言。

through…language 是 process planning 的非限制性定语从句，说明工艺设计的作用。

4. The bills of materials can come directly from the CAD system, which include the stock number, name of item, quantity in stock, unit of measure, minimum stock level, lead time of purchased or manufactured in-house, and the specifications of each component part and suppliers.

物料清单可以直接从 CAD 系统中获得，清单中的信息包括库存号、目录名、库存量、计算单位、最小库存量、外购或自制的提前时间和每个零件和供应商的具体说明。

which…suppliers 是 the bills of materials 的非限制性定语从句，说明清单的内容。

5. Robots are widely used in automated assembly operations for circular and linear transfer.

用于自动装配操作的机械手(工业机器人)主要进行盘式和直线式的传输。

6. CIM encompasses many of the other advanced manufacturing technologies such as CNC, CAD/CAM, robotics and just-in-time delivery.

CIM(计算机集成制造)包含许多先进的制造技术，例如 CNC(计算机数控)、CAD/CAM、工业机器人技术和即时交货技术等。

New Words and Expressions

accuracy [ˈækjurəsi] n. 精确性，准确性
recall [riˈkɔːl] v. 调用，记起，回想
enhance [inˈhɑːns] v. 增强，提高
modification [ˌmɔdifiˈkeiʃən] n. 更改，修正
ease [iːz] v. 使……轻松，安逸
　　　　　　n. 悠闲，不费力
complex [ˈkɔmpleks] adj. 复杂的，合成的

accurate [ˈækjurit] adj. 精确的，正确的
allocate [ˈæləukeit] v. 分配，分派
digit [ˈdidʒit] n. 数字
reference [ˈrefrəns] n. 参考，提及，涉及
bill [bil] n. 清单，账单，票据，议案
lead time 提前时间
in-house 自制的

Project 5　The Computers' Applications in Industry

incorporate [in'kɔːpəreit] v. 合并，混合
dynamic [dai'næmik] adj. 动态的，动力的
machining sequences 工序
verify ['verifai] v. 校验，核实
potential [pə'tenʃ(ə)l] adj. 潜在的，可能的
detect [di'tekt] v. 发觉，侦查，探测
gross [grəus] adj. 粗略的，毛的，大致的
wax [wæks] n. 石蜡
generate ['dʒenə,reit] v. 产生
realistic [riə'listik] adj. 现实的
simulation [,simju'leiʃən] n. 仿真，模拟
critical ['kritikəl] adj. 关键的，临界的，苛刻的
consistent [kən'sistənt] adj. 一致的，坚固的

specification [,spesifi'keiʃən] n. 规格，说明书
assembly [ə'sembli] n. 装配，集合，汇集
approach [ə'prəutʃ] n. 方法，途径，通路
encompass [in'kʌmpəs] v. 包围，环绕
just-in-time delivery [di'livəri] 即时交货
instantaneous [,instən'teinjəs] adj. 即时的
sequence ['siːkwəns] v. 生成程序，使程序化
domain [dəu'mein] n. 范围，领域
fixed automation 刚性自动化
flexible ['fleksəbl] adj. 灵活的
tailor ['teilə] v. 裁剪，适应
hybrid ['haibrid] n. 混合　adj. 混合的

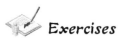

Exercises

Translate the following phrases into Chinese.

1. CNC _____ 　2. CAD _____ 　3. CAM _____
4. CIM _____ 　5. FMS _____ 　6. CAPP _____
7. fixed automation _____ 　8. cutting simulation _____ 　9. lead time _____

Project 6

Manufacturing Technology of Die/Mold

Task 6.1 The Applications of NC/CNC

Numerical Control (NC) is a machining process in which the operations are executed automatically in sequences as specified by the program that contains the information for the tool movements.[1] The NC concept was proposed in the late 1940s by John Parsons of Traverse City, Michigan.

When Numerical Control is performed under computer supervision, it is called Computer Numerical Control (CNC). For both NC and CNC systems, work principles are the same. Only the way in which the execution is controlled is different. Computers are the control units of CNC machines, they are built in or linked to the machines via communications channels.[2] When a programmer input some information in the program by tape and so on, the computer calculates all necessary data to get the job done.

Since its introduction, NC technology has found many applications, including lathes and turning centers, milling machines and machining centers, punches, electrical discharge machines (EDM), flame cutters, grinders, and testing and inspection equipment. One of the most complex CNC machine tools is the turning center, shown in Fig. 6.1 (A modem turning center with a ten-station turret that accepts quick-change tools. Each tool can be positioned in seconds with the press of a button).[3] And the machining center is shown in Fig. 6.2 (Vertical machining center, the tool magazine is on the left of the machine. The control panel on the right can be swiveled by

execute 执行，完成
sequence 顺序，程序
specify 指定
propose 提议，计划
supervision 监控
EDM 电火花加工

via 经过，通过
channel 通道，频道

lathe 车床
turning center 车削中心
milling 铣
machining center 加工中心
punch 冲床，冲孔
flame cutter 线切割
grinder 磨床
turret 转塔刀架
panel 面板

the operator) and Fig. 6.3 (Horizontal machining center, equipped with an automatic tool changer. Tool magazines can store 200 cutting tools).

swivel 旋转
tool magazine 刀库

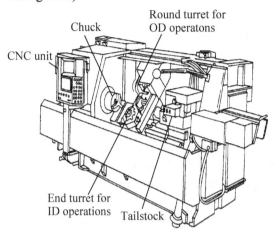

Fig. 6.1 A modern turning center
with a ten-station turret that accepts quick-change tools

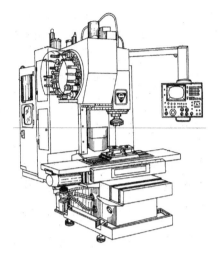

Fig. 6.2 A vertical-spindle machine center

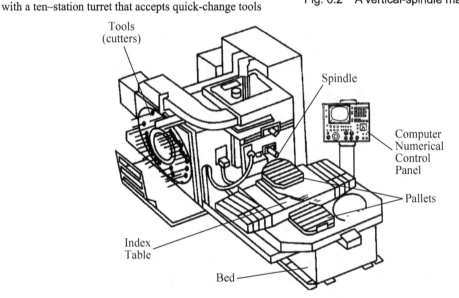

Fig. 6.3 A horizontal-spindle machine center

When preparing a program for a particular operation, the programmer must select all cutting data using recommendations for conventional machining. This includes proper selection of cutting speeds, feed rate, tools and tool geometry, and so on. When the programmer has chosen all of the necessary information properly, the operator loads the program into the machine and presses a button to start the cutting cycle. The CNC machine moves automatically from one machining operation to another, changing the cutting tools and applying the coolant. In a

recommendation 推荐
conventional 惯例的
feed rate 进给率

coolant 冷却液

surprisingly short time, the work-piece is machined according to the highest quality standards. Furthermore, no matter how big the work series is, all of the parts will be almost identical in size and surface finishing. At this time of advanced technology, with its high demands for surface finishing and tolerances of components in, for example, aerospace, nuclear, and medical equipment manufacturing, only CNC machines provide successful results.

tolerance 公差
aerospace 航空
nuclear 核能的

Notes

1. Numerical Control (NC) is a machining process in which the operations are executed automatically in sequences as specified by the program that contains the information for the tool movements.

数字控制是按照含有机床刀具运动信息的程序所指定的顺序自动执行操作的加工过程。

as specified by the program that contains the information for the tool movements 是 sequences 的后置定语，其中 that contains the information for the tool movements 是 the program 的定语从句。

2. Computers are the control units of CNC machines, they are built in or linked to the machines via communications channels.

计算机是 CNC 机床的控制单元，它们内嵌在计算机中或通过通信通道与数控机床连接。

3. The most complex CNC machine tools is the turning center, shown in Fig. 6.1 (A modem turning center with a ten-station turret that accepts quick-change tools. Each tool can be positioned in seconds with the press of a button).

最复杂的计算机数控机床是车削中心，如图 6.1 所示(一个具有十转位的刀架能进行快速换刀的现代车削中心，按下按钮后，可在数秒内定位每个刀具)。

New Words and Expressions

execute [ˈeksikjuːt] v. 执行，完成，实行
sequence [ˈsiːkwəns] n. 顺序，程序，次序
specify [ˈspesifai] v. 指定，详细说明
propose [prəˈpəuz] v. 提议，计划
supervision [ˌsjuːpəˈviʒən] n. 监控，监督
EDM 电火花加工
via [ˈvaiə] prep. 经过，通过
channel [ˈtʃænl] n. 通道，频道，海峡 v. 引导
lathe [leið] n. 车床
turning center 车削中心
milling [ˈmiliŋ] n. 铣

flame cutter 线切割
grinder [ˈgraində] n. 磨床
turret [ˈtʌrit] n. 转塔刀架，车床的刀具转塔
panel [ˈpænl] n. 面板，嵌板，仪表板
swivel [ˈswivl] v. 旋转
magazine [ˌmægəˈziːn] n. 刀库，杂志
recommendation [ˌrekəmenˈdeiʃən] n. 推荐
conventional [kənˈvenʃənl] adj. 惯例的
feed rate 进给率
coolant [ˈkuːlənt] n. 冷却液
tolerance [ˈtɔlərəns] n. 公差，容忍，宽容
aerospace [ˈɛərəuspeis] n. 航空

machining center 加工中心
punch [pʌntʃ] n. 冲床，冲头 v. 冲孔

nuclear ['njuːkliə] adj. 核能的，原子能的

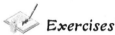

I. Translate the following phrases into Chinese or English.

1. 加工中心 _____   2. 车床 _____   3. 铣床_____
4. numerical control _____   5. 通信渠道 _____   6. 换刀_____

II. Translate the following sentences into Chinese.

When preparing a program for a particular operation, the programmer must select all cutting data using recommendations for conventional machining. This includes proper selection of cutting speeds, feed rate, tools and tool geometry, and so on. When the programmer has chosen all of the necessary information properly, the operator loads the program into the machine and presses a button to start the cutting cycle.

Task 6.2　NC Operation Control Panel

1. Emergency Stop (E-STOP, shown as Fig.6.4)

If this button is pressed, the feed and rotation of the tool is stopped and the control system of the computer is turned off. The E-STOP button is only used in special situations, such as the overloading of the machine, a machined part's loose or incorrect data in the program causing a collision between the tool and the workpiece. To reset the E-STOP button, push it in and turn it clockwise. Then you can turn the machine on, zero it, and eliminate the cause that forced the use of the E-STOP button.

E-STOP 紧急制动
button 按钮，纽扣

overloading 过载，超负荷
collision 冲突，碰撞

clockwise 顺时针

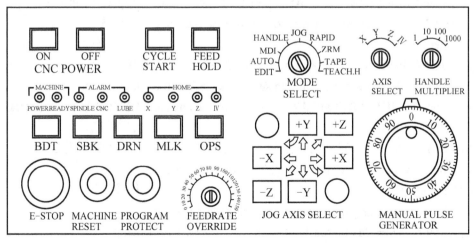

Fig. 6.4　A operation control panel

2. Mode Select

The position of this switch specify the operational mode—whether the computer control or the manual control.

(1) **EDIT** mode enables you to: enter the program to machine memory; enter any changes to the program; transfer data from the program to a tape; check the memory storage capacity.

(2) **AUTO** mode enables the NC commands stored in the memory to be executed.

(3) **MDI** mode enables the automatic control of the machine using information entered in the form of blocks without interfering with the basic program. This is often used during the machining of workpiece holding equipment. It corresponds to single moves such as milling surfaces and drilling holes, descriptions of which need not to be entered to memory storage.[1]

MDI can also be used during the execution of the program. For example, suppose you have omitted the command S350 M03 in the program. In order to correct this omission, turn on the **SINGLE BLOCK** switch **(SBK)** and the position selector switch to the MDI mode.

(4) **HANDLE** mode allows for the manual control of the movements of the machine table with the use of the handwheel **(MANUAL PULSE GENERATOR)**, along one of four axes: *X, Y, Z* or *B*. By turning the handwheel clockwise, you can displace the tool in a positive direction with respect to the position of the coordinate system. Handling the machine manually, use the additional speed switch **(HANDLE MULTIPLIER)**, which can change the value of displacement equal to one skip on the scale of the handwheel.[2]

(5) **JOG** mode allows the selection of manual monotonous feeds along the X, Y, and Z axis. With the selector switch in the JOG mode, use the **JOG AXIS SELECT** buttons, as well as the **FEEDRATE OVERRIDE** switch.

(6) **ZRM** mode is on and then pressing buttons X, Y, or Z causes the machine to return to the zero position for each axis.

3. Cycle Start

Use this button during the execution of the program from memory or tape. When this button is pressed, the control lamp located above it goes on.

模式选择
specify 指定，说明
mode 模式，样式
EDIT 编辑

tape 磁带，录音带

AUTO 自动

MDI 人工数据输入
block 程序段
interfere 干涉，打扰
correspond 符合，协调
description 描述，描写

omit/omission 遗漏，疏忽

SBK 单程序段

HANDLE 手动
table 工作台
handwheel 手轮，驾驶盘
manual pulse generator
手动脉冲发生器
positive 正的，积极的
displacement 位移
skip 跳动
scale 刻度
JOG 点动进给
monotonous 单一的
FEEDRATE OVERRIDE
进给倍率
ZRM 零点返回

循环开始

lamp 灯

4. Feed Hold

When this button is pressed, the control lamp located above it goes on, and the control lamp located above the **CYCLE START** button goes off. When this button is pressed, all feeds are interrupted; however, the rotations are not affected. This button is used very rarely. During the execution of the threading cycle, **FEED HOLD** comes into effect after the tap is withdrawn.[3] If the tap breaks during the threading cycle, the only way to stop the machine is by pressing the **E-STOP** button.

5. Single Block (SBK)

The execution of a single block of information is initiated by turning **SBK** switch on. Each time the **CYCLE START** button is pressed, only one block of information will be executed. This switch can also be used if you intended to check the performance of a new program on the machine or if the momentary interruption of a machine's work is necessary.[4]

6. Dry Run

By turning this switch on, all the rapid and work feeds are changed to one chosen feed. In order to do this, use **FEEDRATE OVERRIDE** and **DRY RUN** to check a new program on the machine without any work actually being performed by the tool.

7. Feedrate Override

This switch allows the control of the work feeds defined function F. You can increase or decrease the percentage of the value entered in the program.

8. Machine Lock (MLK)

This switch is used to check a new program on the machine. All movements of the tool are blocked, while a check is run on the computer screen.

9. CNC Power On / Off

The control is always turned on after the main power switch, located on the door of the control system, is on. The control is always turned off before the main power switch is turned off.

10. Machine Reset

This button is used for cancellation of alarm or an operation. The reset button should not be used while the machine is in working mode.

11. Control Panel

This button is often located at the front of the main electronic system and is equipped with a screen and with various buttons and switches (Fig. 6.5).

12. Display

All the characters, addresses and data are shown on the screen (Fig. 6.6). The contents of the currently active program are active sequence number displayed (Fig. 6.7). In addition, the next schedule and the program list are displayed by the programs.

控制面板

显示

active 现行的，活跃的

schedule 进度，程序表

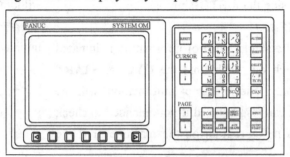

Fig. 6.5　Control Panel (FANUC System)

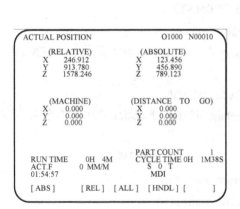

Fig. 6.6　Addresses display

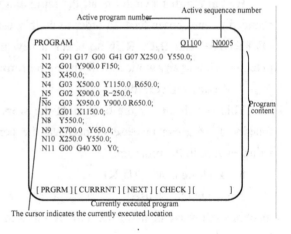

Fig. 6.7　Active program display

 Notes

1. It corresponds to single moves such as milling surfaces and drilling holes, descriptions of which need not be entered to memory storage.

人工数据输入适于像铣平面和钻孔这样的单一加工运动，其描述信息不需要输入到内存中。

descriptions of which need not…storage 是 single moves 的非限制性定语从句。

Project 6 Manufacturing Technology of Die/Mold

2. Handling the machine manually, use the additional speed switch (HANDLE MULTIPLIER), which can change the value of displacement equal to one skip on the scale of the handwheel.

在手动操作机床时，使用附加速度开关(手动变速钮)可改变手动转轮每个刻度的位移量。

3. During the execution of the threading cycle, FEED HOLD comes into effect after the tap is withdrawn.

在加工螺纹时，当丝锥抽出后 FEED HOLD(进给锁定)生效。

come into effect 意为"起作用，生效"。

4. This switch can also be used if you intended to check the performance of a new program on the machine or if the momentary interruption of a machine's work is necessary.

此开关还可以被用在以下两种情况下：用户想在机床上对一段新程序的执行情况进行检查，或在机床加工过程中短暂中断。

本句有两个由 if 引导的并列条件状语从句。

New Words and Expressions

emergency [i'mə:dʒnsi] n. 紧急情况
button ['bʌtn] n. 按钮，纽扣 v. 扣住，扣紧
overloading ['əuvə'ləudiŋ] n. 过载，超负荷
collision [kə'liʒən] n. 冲突，碰撞
clockwise ['klɔkwaiz] adj. & adv. 顺时针
specify ['spesifai] v. 指定，说明
mode [məud] n. 模式，样式，方式，时尚
block [blɔk] n. 程序段，块状物 v. 阻塞，妨碍
interfere [,intə'fiə] v. 干涉，打扰
correspond [kɔris'pɔnd] v. 符合，协调
description [dis'kripʃən] n. 描述，描写
omit [əu'mit] v. 遗漏，疏忽(omission)
handle ['hændl] v. 手动，操作，处理 n. 手柄
table ['teibl] n. 工作台，桌子，平台，表格
handwheel ['hændwi:l] n. 手轮，驾驶盘
Manual Pulse Generator 手动脉冲发生器
positive ['pɔzətiv] adj. 正的，积极的

displacement [dis'pleismənt] n. 位移，取代
skip [skip] n. 跳动，跳跃，蹦
scale [skeil] n. 刻度，比例，天平，等级
jog [dʒɔg] n. 点动进给，轻推，轻撞，漫步
monotonous [mə'nɔtənəs] adj. 单一的，单调的
lamp [læmp] n. 灯 v. 照亮
interrupt [,intə'rʌpt] v. 中断，打断
affect [ə'fekt] v. 影响，感动，侵袭，假装
rarely ['reəli] adv. 很少地，罕有的
threading ['θrediŋ] n. 车螺纹
withdraw [wið'drɔ:] v. 退出，撤退
initiate [i'niʃieit] v. 开动，发动
momentary ['məuməntəri] adj. 瞬时的
dry run 空运行
actually ['æktʃuəli] adv. 实际上，事实上
cancellation [kænsə'leiʃən] n. 取消
reset ['ri:set] v. 复位，重新设置
active ['æktiv] adj. 现行的，活跃的，主动的
schedule [skedju:l] n. 进度，程序表

Exercises

I. Translate the following phrases into English or Chinese.

1. 手动数据输入 _____   2. 工件夹紧装置 _____

3. 单步运行 _____ 4. 空运行 _____ 5. threading cycle _____

6. momentary contact _____ 7. table feed _____ 8. single block _____

II. Interpretation of words and phrases underlined.

1. This is often used during the machining of workpiece holding equipment.

 A. clamping device   B. secessions

 C. plumbing   D. chipper

2. Handling the machine manually, use the additional speed switch (handle multiplier), which can change the value of displacement equal to one skip on the scale of the handwheel.

 A. movement   B. position

 C. increment   D. charge in position

3. During the execution of the threading cycle, FEED HOLD comes into effect after the tap is withdrawn.

 A. comes into existence   B. comes into operation

 C. comes into action   D. comes into being

4. The execution of a single block of information is initiated by turning SBK switch on.

 A. ceased   B. started   C. sponsored   D. pioneered

5. This switch can also be used if you intended to check the performance of a new program on the machine or if the momentary interruption of a machine's work is necessary.

 A. pause in a short time   B. pause for a long time

 C. arbitrary stop   D. temporary trouble

Task 6.3   NC/CNC Machines' Screen Display Reading

  Screen reading is an important skill that can be developed only through experience. This skill is especially needed when proving the program and machining the first part. Many serious problems can be avoided through screen reading.[1]

  There are different screen displays on the monitor of a CNC machine: program screen, position screen, offset screen, work zero screen, and parameter screen.

  Each of these screen displays provides valuable information about the status of the machine tool. But the most important screens for the operator are the offset and position screens. If the machine has work shift capabilities, the work shift screen is also important to performing machine setup.[2]

  1. Offset Screen

  The lathe offset is similar to all lathes. Also, the machining center offset screen is similar to all machining centers. Following (Table 6-1) is the first page of the offset screen taken from one popular machining center.

especially 尤其，特别
prove 证明，检验
program screen 编程屏幕
position screen 位置屏幕
work zero screen
工作零点屏幕
parameter screen 参数屏幕
offset screen
刀具偏置屏幕
work shift screen
加工模式转换屏幕

Table 6-1 Tool Offset

No.	Length		Radius	
	Geometry	Wear	Geometry	Wear
001	−19.1900	0.0000	0.0000	0.0000
002	−20.1300	−0.0100	0.0000	0.0000
003	−17.9000	0.0000	0.0000	0.0000
004	−20.7300	0.0000	0.0000	0.0000
005	19.8820	0.0000	0.0000	0.0000
...	...	...	...	...
015	−12.5770	0.0000	0.5000	0.0050
016	−10.2250	0.0000	0.3750	0.0000

At top is the name of the screen. The screen is divided into two parts: Length and Radius. These are short for tool length offset and tool geometry offset. The tool offset numbers are listed from 1 to 16. Geometry shows the offset entered when the setup was made, and wear shows the tool offset adjustment during machining.

divide 分开，隔开

wear 磨损，穿，戴

The geometry offset number 002 has the value of -20.1300, and an incremental offset adjustment value of -0.01. Thus, the total value of this offset is 20.1310. Note that the geometry offset may also be adjusted in incremental mode. Then the wear offset would be zero. This means that if an offset adjustment is needed, it should be made in geometry or wear, but not in both (it is better to use wear).

incremental 增加的

Offset number 015 has a value of 0.50000 in Radius offset and 0.0050 in wear. This means that this program uses a 0.5 inch tool radius for geometry offset. The offset was adjusted for 0.005 inch during machining. Also, the adjustment can be made in geometry by entering 0.5050. Then the value in wear should be changed to zero. Again, better to use wear.

2. Position Screen

The position screens are very similar to all of the controls. Following (Table 6-2) is the position screen taken from one popular type of lathe.

Table 6-2 Position

Relative	Absolute
U 0.0000	X 15.5720
W 0.0000	Z 5.0210
Machine	distance To Go
X 0.000	X 0.0000
Z -749.300	Z 0.0000

The values in the relative position express the relative tool distance from the home position. This distance is shown in the relative or incremental coordinates, U and W. When reading the values in the relative position, it is not possible to know directly how far the tool is from the part origin, just how far it is from the home position. The sign of the coordinates is zero or negative because the tool cannot move farther than the machine origin. Thus, at present, the values are zero, so the tool is at the home position. The values in the Relative position are normally used when setting up the tools in order to find the real tool distances from the part origin.

relative 相对的

coordinates 坐标
origin 原点

negative 负的

The values in the absolute position express the absolute tool distance from the part origin. This distance is shown in absolute coordinates, X and Z. The sign may be positive or negative, depending on the quadrants in which the tool is moving.³ This is an important piece of information for the operator when machining, since any value in the absolute position is directly related to the part.

absolute 绝对的

positive 正的
quadrant 象限

Notes

1. Screen reading is an important skill that can be developed only through experience. This skill is especially needed when proving the program and machining the first part. Many serious problems can be avoided through screen reading.

屏幕阅读是一项重要技能，并且只有通过实践才能提高。当验证程序和加工第一个零件时，特别需要这项技能。通过屏幕阅读可避免许多严重的问题。

2. Each of these screen displays provides valuable information about the status of the machine tool. But the most important screens for the operator are the offset and position screens. If the machine has work shift capabilities, the work shift screen is also important to performing machine setup.

每一种屏幕显示都提供了许多关于机床状况的有用信息。对于操作者最重要的屏幕是刀具偏置和位置屏幕。如果机床具有加工模式转换功能，则加工模式转换屏幕对于机床设置也是重要的。

3. The sign may be positive or negative, depending on the quadrants in which the tool is moving.

坐标值符号是正还是负取决于刀具在哪个象限运动。

New Words and Expressions

especially [is'peʃəli] adv. 尤其，特别
prove [pru:v] v. 证明，检验，原来是……
parameter [pə'ræmitə] n. 参数
offset [ˌɔf'set] n. & v. 偏置，偏移

relative ['relətiv] adj. 相对的
coordinate [kəu'ɔ:dinit] n. 坐标，同等物
origin ['ɔridʒin] n. 原点
negative ['negətiv] adj. 负的

divide [di'vaid] v. 分开，隔开
wear [wɛə] v. 磨损，穿，戴
incremental [ˌinkri'mentəl] adj. 增加的

absolute ['æbsəlu:t] adj. 绝对的
quadrant ['kwɔdrənt] n. 象限

Exercises

Say true or false to the following statements.

1. Screen reading is an important skill that can be developed only through reading. (   )
2. Many serious problems can be avoided through screen reading. (   )
3. Not every screen provides valuable information about the status of the machine tool. (   )
4. The machining center offset screen is similar to all machining centers. (   )
5. The position screens are different from all of the controls. (   )
6. When reading the values in the relative position, it is possible to know directly how far the tool is from the part origin. (   )
7. The values in the absolute position express the absolute tool distance from the part origin. (   )

Task 6.4   NC Programming

1. Coordinate System for NC Machines

In an NC system, each axis of motion is equipped with a separate driving source that replaces the hand wheel of the conventional machine. The driving source can be DC motor, a stepping motor, or a hydraulic actuator. The source selected is determined mainly based on the precision requirements of the machine.[1]

The relative movement between tools and workpieces is achieved by the motion of the machine tool slides. The three main axes of motion are referred to as the *X*, *Y*, and *Z* axes. The *Z* axis is perpendicular to both the *X* and *Y* axes in order to create a right-hand coordinate system. A positive motion in the Z direction moves the cutting tool away from the workpiece.[2] This is detailed as follows (Fig. 6.8):

(1) *Z* axis

① On a workpiece-rotating machine, such as a lathe, the *Z* axis is parallel to the spindle, and the positive motion moves the tool away from the workpiece.

② On a tool-rotating machine, such as a milling or boring machine, the *Z* axis is perpendicular to the tool set, and the positive motion moves the tool away from the workpiece.

coordinate 坐标

separate 单独的
driving 驱动的
DC motor 直流电机
stepping motor 步进电机
hydraulic actuator 液压传动装置
achieve 完成，达到
slide 工作台，滑板
perpendicular 垂直的
positive 正的
detail 详述，细说

lathe 车床
parallel 平行的
spindle 主轴
milling 铣
boring 镗

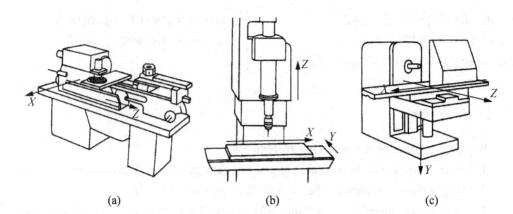

Fig. 6.8 The coordinate system

(a) Lather; (b) Driller; (c) Miller

③ On other machines, such as a press, a planning machine, or shearing machine, the Z axis is perpendicular to the tool set, and the positive motion increases the distance between the tool and the workpiece.

(2) X axis

① On a lathe, the X axis is the direction of tool movement, and positive motion moves the tool away from the workpiece.

② On a horizontal milling machine, the X axis is parallel to the table.

③ On a vertical milling machine, the positive X axis points to the right when the programmer is facing the machine.

(3) Y axis

Y axis is the axis left in a standard Cartesian Coordinate system.

2. Basic Functions of NC Machine Control

To control a machine, it is necessary to begin by defining the coordinates of the tool motion and to specify whether the motion is a positioning motion (rapid traverse) or a feed motion (cutting). The feed motion includes linear motion and circular motion. Linear motion requires the destination coordinates. When circular interpolation is used, the center of the circle and the destination must be given.

Before a cutting motion is called out, the spindle must be turned to the desired rpm and the feed speed must be specified. The spindle can rotate either clockwise or counterclockwise.

Sometimes coolant is required in machining, and the coolant may be applied in fluid or mist form.

If an automatic tool changer is present, the tool number has to be known to the controller before a tool can be changed to the machine spindle.[3] The sequence to change the tool also needs to be specified.

planning 刨
shearing 剪

horizontal 水平的

vertical 垂直的

function 功能，函数

position 定位，位置
rapid traverse 快速横向运动
destination 目标，终点
interpolation 插补
call out 调用
rpm 转数/分
counterclockwise 逆时针
coolant 冷却液
mist 薄雾

It is often desirable to aggregate a fixed sequence of operations such as drilling holes into a cycle.[4] Using cycle codes can drastically reduce programming effort. Additional information is needed for specific cycle operations.

Finally, there are other programming functions, such as units-inch or metric, positioning system-absolute or incremental, and so on. All of these activities can and in some cases must be controlled through the NC controller and related part program.

These control functions are summarized in the followings.

(1) Preparatory Functions specify units, which interpolator, absolute or incremental programming, which circular interpolation plane, cutter compensation, and so on.

(2) Coordinates define three dimensional (and three rotational) axes.

(3) Machining Parameters specify feed and speed.

(4) Tool Control specifies tool diameter, next tool number, tool change, and so on.

(5) Cycle Functions specify drill cycle, ream cycle, born cycle, mill cycle, and clearance plane.

(6) Coolant Control specifies the coolant condition, that is, coolant on/off, fluid/mist.

(7) Miscellaneous control specifies all other control specifics, that is, spindle on/off, tape rewind, spindle rotation direction, pallet change, clamps control, and so on.

(8) Interpolators specify linear, circular, or circle center interpolation.

These control functions are programmed through program codes.

(1) G-Code is also called preparatory code or word. It is used to prepare the MCU for control functions (Table 6-3).

aggregate 集合，聚集
cycle 循环
drastically 剧烈地
inch 英制
metric 米制
absolute 绝对的
incremental 增量的
activity 行为
准备功能
cutter compensation 刀具补偿
坐标
加工参数
刀具控制
specify 指定，说明
循环功能
冷却液控制
specific 细节
辅助控制
tape rewind 磁带重绕
pallet 托盘，棘爪
clamp 夹具，夹紧
interpolation 插补
code/word 代码，指令
MCU 机床控制装置

Table 6-3 Some commonly used G-Codes

G00	rapid traverse 快速定位，快速横向运动		G40	cutter compensation-cancel 刀补取消
G01	linear interpolation 直线插补		G41	cutter compensation-left 刀具补偿-左刀补
G02	circular interpolation, CW 圆弧插补，顺时针		G42	cutter compensation-right 刀具补偿-右刀补
G03	circular interpolation, CCW 圆弧插补，逆时针		G43	cutter offset positive 刀具正偏值
G04	dwell 暂停		G44	cutter offset negative 刀具负偏值
G08	acceleration 加速		G80	fixed-cycle cancel 固定循环取消
G09	deceleration 减速		G81~89	fixed cycles 固定循环
G17	X-Y plane XY平面		G90	absolute dimension program 绝对坐标编程
G18	Z-X Plane ZX平面		G91	incremental dimension 增量坐标编程
G19	Y-Z Plane YZ平面		G92	set the workpiece origin 设定工件原点
G20	inch format 英制格式		G96	constant surface speed control 恒线速控制
G21	metric format 米制格式		G97	constant spindle speed control 恒转速控制
G28	return to reference point 返回参考点		G98	feed per minute 每分钟进给
G33	thread cutting 螺纹切削		G99	feed per revolution 每转进给

(2) **F-Code** specifies the feed speed of the tool motion. It is the relative speed between the cutting tool and the workpiece. It is typically specified in in/min. Feed speed can be changed frequently in a program, as needed.

frequently 经常地

(3) **S-Code** is the cutting-speed code. Cutting speed is the specification of the relative surface speed of the cutting edge with respect to the workpiece. It is the result of the tool or the workpiece rotation. Therefore, it is programmed in rpm. Some handbooks give these values in surface feet per minute (sfpm), and conversion is required before programming is done.[5] When a controller is equipped with a sfpm programming option, the operator must specify the tool diameter. The S-Code is specified before the spindle is turned on. The S-Code does not turn on the spindle. The spindle is turned on by an M-Code.

specification 说明
with respect to 关于
conversion 转化
option 选项，选择

(4) **T-Code** is used to specify the tool number. It is used only when an automatic tool changer is present. It specifies the slot number on the tool magazine in which the next tool is located. Actual tool change does not occur until a tool change M-Code is specified.

slot 位置，缝

(5) **R-Code** is used for cycle parameter. When a drill cycle is specified, one must give a clearance height(R plane). The R-Code is used to specify this clearance height.

(6) **M-Code** is called the miscellaneous word and is used to control miscellaneous functions of the machine. Such functions (Table 6-4) include turn the spindle on/off, start/stop the machine, turn on/off the coolant, change the tool, and rewind the program tape.

miscellaneous 多方面的

Table 6-4   M-Codes

M00	program stop 程序停止	M08	mist coolant on 雾冷状态冷却液开
M01	optional stop 选择性停止	M09	coolant off 冷却液关
M02	end of program 程序结束	M10	chuck close 卡盘夹紧
M03	spindle cw 主轴顺时针转	M11	chuck open 卡盘松开
M04	spindle ccw 主轴逆时针转	M30	end of tape 磁带程序结束
M05	spindle stop 主轴停止	M98	calling of subprogram 调用子程序
M06	tool change 换刀	M99	end of subprogram (return to main program) 子程序结束，返至主程序
M07	fluid coolant on 液冷状态冷却液开		

Notes

1. The source selected is determined mainly based on the precision requirements of the machine.
选用何种驱动源主要根据机床的精度要求来确定。
based on the precision requirements of the machine 为方式状语。

2. A positive motion in the Z axis moves the cutting tool away from the workpiece.
Z轴的正向定义为刀具离开工件的方向。

3. If an automatic tool changer is present, the tool number has to be known to the controller before a tool can be changed to the machine spindle.
在带有自动换刀装置的机床上，一把刀具被安装到机床主轴上之前，必须将其编号输入给控制器。

4. It is often desirable to aggregate a fixed sequence of operations such as drilling holes into a cycle.
现在倾向于将一些类似钻孔这样具有固定工序的操作集合在一个循环内。
本句为"it (形式主语) + is + adj.(表语)+ to do...(真正主语)"句型，原译为"……是人们所期望的。"
aggregate…into=come…together。

5. Some handbooks give these values in surface feet per minute (sfpm.), and conversion is required before programming is done.
一些(机床加工数据)手册中给出的数据单位为"每分钟表面英尺数"(sfpm.)，编程前必须进行转换。

New Words and Expressions

coordinate [kəu'ɔːdinit] n. 坐标，同等物
separate ['sepəreit] adj. & v. 单独，隔离，独立
driving ['draiviŋ] adj. 驱动的 n. 操作，驾驶
DC = direct current 直流
motor ['məutə] n. 电机，马达，发动机
stepping ['stepiŋ] n. 步进，分级
hydraulic [hai'drɔːlik] adj. 液压的，水力的
actuator ['æktjueitə] n. 传动装置，执行机构
achieve [ə'tʃiːv] v. 完成，达到
slide ['slaid] n. 工作台，滑板，拖板
perpendicular [ˌpəːpən'dikjulə] adj. 垂直的
detail ['diːteil] v. 详述，细说
lathe ['leið] n. 车床
spindle ['spindl] n. 主轴

rpm = revolutions per minute 转数/分
counterclockwise [ˌkauntə'klɔkwaiz] 逆时针
coolant ['kuːlənt] n. 冷却液，冷冻剂，散热剂
mist [mist] n. 薄雾
aggregate ['æɡriɡeit] adj. n. & v. 集合，聚集
cycle ['saikl] n. & v. 循环，周期
drastically ['dræstikəli] adv. 剧烈地，彻底地
inch [intʃ] n. 英制，英寸
metric ['metrik] adj. 米制的，公制的
absolute ['æbsəluːt] adj. 绝对的
incremental [inkri'mentəl] adj. 增量的
activity [æk'tiviti] n. 行为，活动，活跃
compensation [kɔmpen'seiʃən] n. 补偿，赔偿
specify ['spesifai] v. 指定，说明，列入清单
specific [spi'sifik] n. 细节 adj. 明确的，特殊的

milling ['miliŋ] n. 铣
boring ['bɔːriŋ] n. 镗
planning ['plæniŋ] n. 刨
shearing ['ʃiəriŋ] n. 剪
horizontal [ˌhɔriˈzɔntl] adj. 水平的，地平线的
vertical ['vəːtikəl] adj. 垂直的，直立的
function ['fʌŋkʃən] n. 功能，函数，职责
position [pəˈziʃən] n. & v. 定位，位置
traverse ['trævə(ː)s] adj. & n. & v. 横向运动，横越
destination [ˌdestiˈneiʃən] n. 目的地，终点
interpolation [inˌtəːpəuˈleiʃən] n. 插补，填写
call out 调用

rewind [riːˈwaind] n. & v. 重绕
pallet ['pælit] n. 托盘，棘爪
clamp [klæmp] n. 夹具，夹子 v. 夹紧
MCU=Machine Control Unit 机床控制装置
=Magnetic Card Unit 磁性卡片装置
=Microprogram Control Unit 微程序控制器
frequently ['friːkwəntli] adv. 经常地，频繁地
specification [ˌspesifiˈkeiʃən] n. 说明，规范
with respect to 关于
conversion [kənˈvəːʃən] n. 转化，变换
option ['ɔpʃən] n. 选项，选择
slot [slɔt] n. 位置，缝，水沟 v. 开槽，跟踪
miscellaneous [misiˈleinjəs] adj. 多方面的

Exercises

I. Say true or false to the following statements.

1. The driving source can be DC motor, a stepping motor, or a hydraulic actuator. (　　)

2. The three main axes of motion are referred to as the *X*, *Y*, and *Z* axes. (　　)

3. On a tool-rotating machine, such as a milling or boring machine, the *Y* axis is perpendicular to the tool set, and the positive motion moves the tool away from the workpiece. (　　)

4. On a horizontal milling machine, the *X* axis is parallel to the table. (　　)

5. To control a machine, it is necessary to begin by defining the coordinates of the tool motion.(　　)

II. Translate the following phrases into English or Chinese.

1. 手轮 _____　　2. 传统机床_____　　3. machine tool slide _____
4. 刀具补偿_____　　5. 直线插补_____　　6. 英制_____
7. 钻削循环_____　　8. 螺纹切削_____　　9. rpm _____

III. Translate the following sentences into Chinese.

1. The source selected is determined mainly based on the precision requirements of the machine.

2. The relative movement between tools and workpieces is achieved by the motion of the machine tool slides.

3. On a vertical milling machine, the positive *X* axis points to the right when the programmer is facing the machine.

4. The T-Code is used to specify the tool number. It is used only when an automatic tool changer is present. It specifies the slot number on the tool magazine in which the next tool is located. Actual tool change does not occur until a tool change M-code is specified.

Project 6 Manufacturing Technology of Die/Mold

Task 6.5 Safety Notes for CNC Machine Operations

Safety is always a major concern in a metal-cutting operation. CNC equipment is automated and very fast, and consequently it is a source of hazards. The hazards have to be located and the personnel must be aware of them in order to prevent injuries and damage to the equipment.[1]

Main potential hazards include: rotating parts, such as the spindle, the tool in the spindle, chuck, part in the chuck, and the turret with the tools and rotating clamping devices; movable parts, such as the machining center table, lathe slides, tailstock center, and tool carousel; errors in the program such as improper use of the G00 code in conjunction with the wrong coordinate value, which can generate an unexpected rapid motion; an error in setting or changing the offset value, which can result in a collision of the tool with the part or the machine; and a hazardous action of the machine caused by unqualified changes in a proven program.

To minimize or avoid hazards, try the following preventive actions.

(1) Keep all of the original covers on the machines as supplied by the machine tool builder.

(2) Wear safety glasses, gloves, and proper clothing and shoes.

(3) Do not attempt to run the machine before you are familiar with its control.

(4) Before running the program, make sure that the part is clamped properly.[2]

(5) When proving a program, follow these safety procedures.

① Run the program using the Machine Lock function to check the program for errors in syntax and geometry.

② Slow down rapid motions using the RAPID OVERRIDE switch or dry run the program.

③ Use a single-block execution to confirm each line in the program before executing it.

④ When the tool is cutting, slow down the feed rate using the FEED OVERRIDE switch to prevent excessive cutting conditions.

(6) Do not handle chips by hand and do not use chip hooks to break long curled chips. Program different cutting conditions for

---

concern 关注
consequently 因此
hazard 危险
locate 查找
injury / damage 伤害
potential 潜在的
chuck 卡盘

slide 拖板
turret 转塔刀架
tailstock 尾座，尾架
carousel 旋转式传送带
conjunction 联合
collision 碰撞
hazardous 危险的
unqualified 不合格的
minimize 最小化
preventive 预防性的

glove 手套

procedure 措施，手续

syntax 语法，句法

RAPID OVERRIDE 快速倍率

execution 执行
confirm 确认

FEED OVERRIDE 进给倍率
handle 处理

better chip control. Stop the machine if you need to properly clean the chips.

(7) If there is any doubt that the insert will break under the programmed cutting conditions, choose a thicker insert or reduce feed or depth of cut.³

(8) Keep tool overhang as short as possible, since it can be a source of vibration that can break the insert.

(9) When supporting a large part by the center, make sure that the hole-center is large enough to adequately support and hold the part.

(10) Stop the machine when changing the tools, indexing inserts, or removing chips.

(11) Replace dull or broken tools or inserts.

(12) Write a list of offsets for active tools, and clear (set to zero) the offsets for tools removed from the machine.

(13) Do not make changes in the program if your supervisor has prohibited your doing so.

(14) If you have any safety-related concerns, notify your instructor or supervisor immediately.

chip 切屑
hook 钩子
curled 卷的
insert 刀片

overhang 悬于……之上
vibration 振动

adequately 充分地

dull 钝的
active 现行的

supervisor 主管
prohibit 禁止

instructor 指导

 Notes

1. The hazards have to be located and the personnel must be aware of them in order to prevent injuries and damage to the equipment.

为了防止对人身造成伤害和对设备造成损坏，必须找出危险所在，而且操作人员必须提高警惕注意这些危险。

have to=must，但 have to 表示客观上必须做某事，must 表示主观上必须做某事。

2. Before running the program, make sure that the part is clamped properly.

运行程序前应确信零件被正确装夹。

3. If there is any doubt that the insert will break under the programmed cutting conditions, choose a thicker insert or reduce feed or depth of cut.

如果怀疑刀片在已编入程序的切削条件下可能会断裂，要选择一个更厚的刀片，或者减少进给或切削深度。

 New Words and Expressions

concern [kən'sə:n] n. 关注，关心 v. 涉及
consequently ['kɔnsikwəntli] adv. 因此，从而

syntax ['sintæks] n. 语法，句法，有秩序的排列 RAPID OVERRIDE 快速倍率

Project 6 Manufacturing Technology of Die/Mold

hazard ['hæzəd] n. 危险 v. 冒险，使……遭危险
locate [ləu'keit] v. 查找，定位，位于
injury ['indʒəri] n. (特指人身)伤害，侮辱
damage ['dæmidʒ] n. 损害，伤害，赔偿金
chuck [tʃʌk] n. 卡盘 v. 用卡盘夹紧
slide ['slaid] n. 拖板，滑板 v.(使)滑动
turret ['tʌrit] n. 转塔刀架，塔楼
tailstock ['teilstɔk] n. 尾座，尾架，顶针座
carousel [,kærə'zel] n. 旋转式传送带
conjunction [kən'dʒʌŋkʃən] n. 联合
collision [kə'liʒən] n. 碰撞，冲突
hazardous ['hæzədəs] adj. 危险的，冒险的
unqualified ['ʌn'kwɔlifaid] adj. 不合格的
minimize ['minimaiz] v. 最小化，将……减到最小
preventive [pri'ventiv] adj. 预防性的
glove [glʌv] n. 手套 v. 戴手套

FEED OVERRIDE 进给倍率
execution [,eksi'kjuːʃən] n. 执行，完成，制作
confirm [kən'fəːm] v. 确认，批准，使有效
handle ['hændl] v. 处理，操作 n. 手柄
chip [tʃip] n. 切屑 v. 削成碎片
hook [huk] n. 钩子 v. 钩住，沉迷
curled [kəːld] adj. 卷曲的，卷缩的
insert [in'səːt] n. 刀片，嵌入物 v. 嵌入，插入
overhang ['əuvə'hæŋ] v. 悬于……之上，悬垂
vibration [vai'breiʃən] n. 振动，摆动，颤动
adequately ['ædikwitli] adv. 充分地
dull [dʌl] adj. 钝的，呆滞的 v. 使变钝，缓和
active ['æktiv] adj. 现行的，积极的，活跃的
supervisor ['sjuːpəvaizə] n. 主管，监督人
prohibit [prə'hibit] v. 禁止，阻止
instructor [in'strʌktə] n. 指导，教员

Exercises

I. Translate the following phrases into English or Chinese.

1. 主轴 _____ 2. 卡盘 _____ 3. 转塔车床 _____ 4. 刀片 _____
5. 机床厂 _____ 6. 坐标值 _____ 7. tailstock center _____
8. at all hazards _____ 9. chip formation _____

II. Translate the following sentences into Chinese.

1. The hazards have to be located and the personnel must be aware of them in order to prevent injuries and damage to the equipment.

2. If there is any doubt that the insert will break under the programmed cutting conditions, choose a thicker insert or reduce feed or depth of cut.

3. Before running the program, make sure that the part is clamped properly.

4. Keep all of the original covers on the machines as supplied by the machine tool builder.

5. CNC equipment is automated and very fast, and consequently it is a source of hazards.

Task 6.6　Fault Diagnosis and Action

When a running fault occurs, examine the correct cause to take proper action. To do this, execute the checks below.

(1) When did the fault occur?

(2) For automatic operation—program number, sequence number, and program contents?

(3) In manual operation or specific mode?

(4) Preceding and succeeding operations?

(5) During I/O operation?

(6) Machine system status?

(7) During tool change?

(8) Display the alarm diagnosis screen to check the contents of alarm.

(9) What does the driving amplifier status display indicate? Check the contents of alarm based on the driving amplifier status display.

(10) What does the machine sequence alarm indicate?

(11) Is the CRT screen normal?

(12) Is the control axis hunting?

(13) Frequency for the same kind of work?

(14) Does the fault occur when the same operation is made? (Repeatability check)

(15) Does the same fault occur when the conditions change ? (Override, program contents, operating procedure, etc.)

1. Fault Example

(1) The power cannot be turned on.

Check the following points:

The power is being supplied?

(2) The NC unit does not operate when being activated.

Check the following points:

① Mode selected normally?

② All conditions for start satisfied? Depending on the machine, the start may be locked until the predetermined conditions are satisfied. Check this by referring to the manual published by the machine manufacturer.

③ Override or manual speed=0?

④ No reset and feed hold signal is being generated.

⑤ Machine lock is on.

---

fault 故障，缺点

preceding 在前的
succeeding 随后的
I/O 开/关，输入/输出
status 状态，情形
diagnosis 诊断

amplifier 放大器
indicate 说明，指出

hunt 搜寻

repeatability 重复性
override 倍率开关

activate 使活动

signal 信号
generate 发生

2. Alarm Message

When the menu key ALARM is pressed, the ALARM/DIAGN screen is displayed.

(1) **Alarm:** The code and number or messages relating to an operation alarm, program error, servo alarm, or system error are displayed.   servo 伺服

(2) **Stop code:** The automation operation disable state or stop state in automatic operation mode is displayed in code and error number.

(3) **Alarm message:** The alarm messages specified by the built-in user PLC are displayed.   built-in 内置的

(4) **Operator message:** The operator messages specified by the built-in user PLC are displayed.

When an alarm occurs, the class code will display on all screens. Refer to the list of alarms for details in the manual published by the machine manufacturer.

New Words and Expressions

fault [fɔːlt] n. 故障，缺点 v. 找毛病，弄错
preceding [pri(ː)'siːdiŋ] adj. 在前的，前述的
succeeding [sək'siːdiŋ] adj. 随后的，以后的
I/O=input/output 开/关，输入/输出
status ['steitəs] n. 状态，情形，身份，地位
diagnosis [ˌdaiəg'nəusis] n. 诊断
amplifier ['æmpliˌfaiə] n. 放大器，扩音器
indicate ['indikeit] v. 说明，指出，象征，显示

hunt [hʌnt] v. & n. 搜寻，打猎，猎取
repeatability [riˌpiːtə'biliti] n. 重复性
override [ˌəuvə'raid] n. 倍率开关
activate ['æktiveit] v. 使活动，刺激，有活力
signal ['signl] n. 信号 adj. 有信号的 v. 发信号
generate ['dʒenəˌreit] v. 发生，产生
servo ['səːvəu] v. 伺服，伺服系统
built-in 内置的

Exercises

I. Say true or false to the following statements.

1. When a running fault occurs, first examine the correct cause and then take proper action. ( )

2. When the power cannot be turned on, check if the power is being supplied. ( )

3. The only reason for the NC unit does not operate when being activated is that no feed hold signal is being generated. ( )

4. If the frequency is too small, or the fault occurred during operation of another machine, the cause must be noises of the supply voltage. ( )

5. When the menu key ALARM is pressed, the ALARM/DIAGN screen is off. ( )

II. Translate the following paragraph into Chinese.

If the frequency is too small, or the fault occurred during operation of another machine, the cause must be noises(干扰)of the supply voltage. In this case, check that the supply voltage is normal. (Does momentary drop occur during operation of another machine?) And then, take the measures against noises.

Task 6.7　Types of Control Devices

Several types of control devices are used in industry to satisfy the following control needs:

Mechanical Control	机械控制
Pneumatic Control	气动控制
Electromechanical Control	机电控制
Electronic Control	电子控制
Computer Control	计算机控制
Programmable Logic Control (PLC)	可编程逻辑控制

Mechanical control includes cams and governors. Although they have been used for the control of very complex machines, to be cost effectively, today they are used for simple and fixed-cycle task control. Some automated machines, such as screw machines, still use cam-based control. Mechanical control is difficult to manufacture and is subject to wear.

cam 凸轮
governor 调速器
effectively 有效地
screw machine 攻螺纹机床

Pneumatic control is still very popular for valves, and switches to construct simple control logic, but is relatively slow. Because standard components are used to construct the logic, it is easier to build than a mechanical control. Pneumatic control parts are subject to wear.

pneumatic 气动的

As does a mechanical control, an electromechanical control uses switches, relays, timers, counters, and so on, to construct logic. Because electric current is used, it is faster and more flexible. The controllers using electromechanical control are called relay devices.

electromechanical 机电的，机电一体化的
switch 开关
relay 继电器
timer 定时器
counter 计时器
component 元件，零件
reliable 可靠的
versatile 通用的
strategy 策略

Electric control is similar to electromechanical control, except that the moving mechanical components in an electromechanical control device are replaced by electronic switches, which works faster and is more reliable.

Computer control is the most versatile control system. The logic of the control is programmed into the computer memory using software. It not only can be for machine and manufacturing system control, but also for data communication. Very complex control strategies with extensive computations can be programmed. The first is the interface with the outside world. Internally, the computer uses a low voltage (5 to 12 volts) and a low current (several milliamps). Machine requires much higher voltages (24,110, or 220 volts) and currents (measured in amps). The interface not only has to convert the voltage difference, but also must filter out the electric noise usually found in the shop. The interface thus must be custom-built for each application.[1]

A PLC(programmable logic controller)was replacement for relay devices. They are programmed using a ladder diagram, which is standard electric wiring diagram. Like a general-purpose computer, a PLC consists of five major parts: CPU (processor), memory, input/output (I/O), power supply, and peripherals (Fig. 6.9). Fig. 6.10 shows a small PLC, which has 16 I/O points and a standard RS-232 serial communication port.

As PLCs become more flexible, high-level as well as low-level languages are available to PLC programmers. PLCs have the flexibility of computers as well as a standard and easy interface with processes and other devices. They are widely accepted in industry for controlling from a single device to a complex manufacturing facility, and from simple process control to manufacturing system controls and monitoring. They are used for high-speed digital processing, high-speed digital communication, high-level compute-language support, and of course, for basic process control.[2] (Fig. 6.11)

extensive 大量的

voltage 电压，伏特数
milliamps 毫安
amps 安培
convert 转换
filter 过滤

replacement 替代物

general-purpose 通用的
processor 处理器
peripheral 外围设备
serial 串行的，串联的
communication 通信
port 端口，港口
flexible 灵活的
available 可用的

facility 设备
monitoring 监视，监测

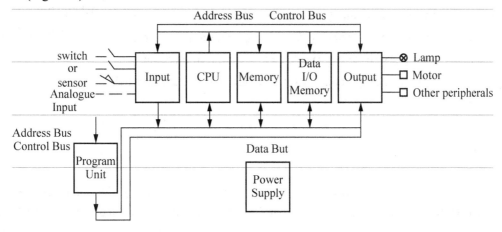

Fig. 6.9 Programmable Controller Architecture

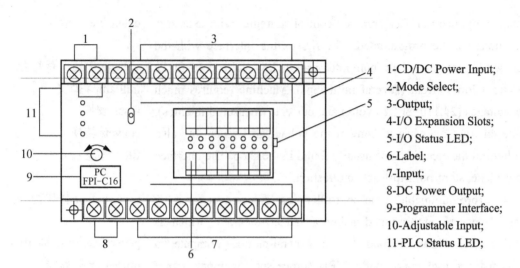

Fig. 6.10　FP1 C16 Control Panel

1-CD/DC Power Input;
2-Mode Select;
3-Output;
4-I/O Expansion Slots;
5-I/O Status LED;
6-Label;
7-Input;
8-DC Power Output;
9-Programmer Interface;
10-Adjustable Input;
11-PLC Status LED;

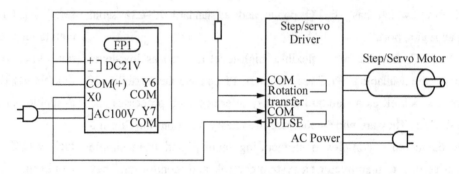

Fig. 6.11　Application of PLC (Controls Step/Servo Motor)

  Breadboarding a relay panel circuit is a tedious task; it requires a lot of careful planning and work. The debugging and changing of a circuit is even more difficult. Programmable logic controllers replace most of this wiring by software programming; therefore, the task is made much easier. Because the wires and the moving mechanical components (relay contacts) are mostly replaced by software, the system is much more reliable.[3]

breadboard 电路试验板路
tedious 单调乏味的
debug 调试
relay contact 继电器触头

 Notes

  1. The first is the interface with the outside world. Internally, the computer uses a low voltage (5 to 12 volts) and a low current (several milliamps). Machine requires much higher voltages (24,110, or 220 voltages) and currents (measured in amps). The interface not only has to convert the voltage difference, but also must filter out the electric noise usually found in the shop. The interface thus must be custom-built for each application.

Project 6 Manufacturing Technology of Die/Mold

首先要解决与外界的接口问题。在控制电路内部计算机使用低电压(5～12V)和小电流(几毫安)，机床的外部电路则需要高电压(24、110 或 220V)和大电流(以安计量)，接口不仅要进行不同电压的转换，而且必须对车间中经常存在的电流干扰加以过滤，这样的接口必须是用户针对不同应用来订做的。

2. They are used for high-speed digital processing, high-speed digital communication, high-level compute-language support, and of course, for basic process control.

它们(PLC)被用于高速数据处理、高速数据通信、高级计算机语言支持，当然也用于基本过程控制。

of course 为插入语，起附加说明的作用。

3. Because the wires, the moving mechanical components, and relay contacts are mostly replaced by software; the system is much more reliable.

由于线路、运动的机械零件和继电器触头大部分被软件所代替，因此(PLC)系统更可靠。

New Words and Expressions

cam [kæm] n. 凸轮，偏心轮，样板，靠模
governor ['gʌvənə] n. 调节器，统治者，变阻器
effectively [i'fektivli] adv. 有效地，有力地
screw machine 螺纹机床
pneumatic [nju(ː)'mætik] adj. 气动的，风力的
electromechanical [i,lektrəumi'kænikəl] adj. 机电的，机电一体化的
switch [switʃ] n. 开关，电闸，转换 v. 转换
relay ['riːlei] n. 继电器，接替 v. 传播
counter ['kauntə] n. 计时器，计数器
component [kəm'pəunənt] n. 元件，零件
reliable [ri'laiəbl] adj. 可靠的，可信赖的
versatile ['vəːsətail] adj. 通用的，多面手的
strategy ['strætidʒi] n. 策略
extensive [iks'tensiv] adj. 大量的，广大的
voltage ['vəultidʒ] n. 电压，伏特数
milliamp ['mili,æmpɛə(r)] n. 毫安
amps=ampere ['æmpɛə(r)] n. 安培

convert [kən'vəːt] v. 转换，改变信仰
filter ['filtə] v. 过滤，筛选，渗透 n. 过滤器
replacement [ri'pleismənt] n. 替代物，交换
general-purpose 通用的
processor ['prəusesə] n. 处理器
peripheral [pə'rifərəl] n. & adj. 外围设备(的)
serial ['siəriəl] adj. 串行的，串联的，连续的
communication [kə,mjuːni'keiʃn] n. 通信
port [pɔːt] n. 端口，港口
flexible ['fleksəbl] adj. 灵活的，柔软的
available [ə'veiləbl] adj. 可用的，可利用的
facility [fə'siliti] n. 设备，容易，灵巧，便利
monitoring ['mɔnitəriŋ] n. 监视，监测
breadboard ['bredbɔːd] n. 电路试验板路，案板
tedious ['tiːdiəs] adj. 单调乏味的，沉闷的
debug [diː'bʌg] v. 调试，除去有毛病的
relay contact 继电器触头
LED = light-emitting diode 发光二极管

Exercises

I. Say true or false to the following statements.

1. Like a general-purpose computer, a PLC consists of six major parts. (   )
2. Programmable logic controllers replace most of this wiring by software programming. (   )
3. PLCs are widely accepted in industry for controlling from a single device to a complex manufacturing facility. (   )
4. Mechanical control includes cams and governors. (   )
5. Mechanical control is difficult to manufacture and is subject to wear. (   )
6. The logic of the control is programmed into the computer memory using hardware. (   )

II. Translate the following phrases into Chinese.

1. PLC _____   2. ladder diagram _____   3. pneumatic control _____
4. screw machine _____   5. filter out _____   6. electronic governor _____
7. electromechanical control _____   8. low voltage _____

III. Translate the following sentences into Chinese.

1. Programmable logic controllers (PLCs) were first introduced in 1968 as a substitute for hardwired relay panels.
2. Because the wires and the moving mechanical components (relay contacts) are mostly replaced by software, the system is much more reliable.
3. They are programmed using a ladder diagram, which is standard electric wiring diagram.

Task 6.8　Non-traditional Manufacturing Processes

Non-traditional manufacturing processes are defined as a group of processes that remove excess material by various techniques involving mechanical, thermal, electrical or chemical energy or combinations of these energies but do not use sharp cutting tools as it needs to be used for traditional manufacturing processes.[1]

non-traditional 特种的
excess 多余，过度

combination 联合

Non-traditional manufacturing processes, also called advanced manufacturing processes, are employed where traditional machining processes, such as turning, drilling, shaping and milling, are not feasible, satisfactory or economical due to special reasons as outlined below.

feasible 可行的

(1) Very hard fragile materials difficult to clamp for traditional machining.

(2) When the workpiece is too flexible or slender.
(3) When the shape of the part is too complex.

flexible 柔软的
slender 薄弱的

1. Electrical Discharge Machining (EDM)

EDM utilizes thermoelectric process to erode undesired materials from the workpiece by a series of discrete electrical sparks between the workpiece and the electrode.[2] So, the hardness of the material is no longer a dominating factor for EDM process. A schematic of an EDM process is shown in Fig. 6.12, where the tool and the workpiece are immersed in a dielectric fluid.

电火花加工
utilize 利用，使用
discrete 不连续，离散
spark 瞬间放电，火花
electrode 电极
dominating 主要的
schematic 示意图
immerse 沉浸，陷入

The EDM process has the ability to machine hard, difficult-to-machine materials. Parts with complex, precise and irregular shapes for forging, press tools, extrusion dies, difficult internal shapes for aerospace and medical applications can be made by EDM process. Some of the shapes made by EDM process are shown in Fig. 6.13.

extrusion die 挤出模

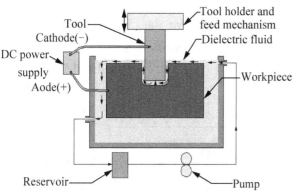

Fig. 6.12 Schematic of EDM process

Fig. 6.13 Difficult internal parts made by EDM

EDM removes material by discharging an electrical current, normally stored in a capacitor bank, across a small gap between the tool-cathode and the workpiece-anode typically in the order of 50volts/10amps. This high voltage induces an electric field in the insulating dielectric that is present in narrow gap between electrode and workpiece. This cause conducting particles suspended in the dielectric to concentrate at the points of strongest electrical field. When the potential difference between the electrode and the workpiece is sufficiently high, the dielectric breaks down and a transient spark discharges through the dielectric fluid, removing small amount of material from the workpiece surface.

discharge 放电
current 电流
capacitor 电容
cathode 阴极，负极
anode 阳极，正极
insulating 绝缘的
dielectric 电介质
suspend 悬挂，吊
potential 潜在的
transient 瞬时的

Dielectric fluids used in EDM process are hydrocarbon oils, kerosene and deionizer water. The functions of the dielectric fluid are to act as an insulator between the tool and the workpiece, coolant, a flushing medium for the removal of the chips. The electrodes for EDM process usually are made of graphite, brass, copper and copper-tungsten alloys.

hydrocarbon 烃
kerosene 煤油
deionizer 脱离子剂
flush 冲洗
tungsten 钨
graphite 石墨

2. Wire EDM

EDM, primarily, exists commercially in the form of die-sinking machines and wire-cutting machines (Fig. 6.14). In wire EDM, a slowly moving wire travels along a prescribed path and removes material from the workpiece. Wire EDM uses electro-thermal mechanisms to cut electrically conductive materials. The material is removed by a series of discrete discharges between the wire electrode and the workpiece in the presence of dielectric fluid, which creates a path for each discharge as the fluid becomes ionized in the gap. The area where discharge takes place is heated to extremely high temperature, so that the surface is melted and removed. The removed particles are flushed away by the flowing dielectric fluids.

The wire EDM process can cut intricate components for the electric and aerospace industries, pattern tool steel for die manufacturing, cut cylindrical objects with high precision.[3]

线切割
die-sinking machine 加工凹模的机床
prescribe 指示，指定

ionize 使离子化，电离

intricate 复杂的
aerospace 航空
cylindrical 圆柱的
precision 准确，精确

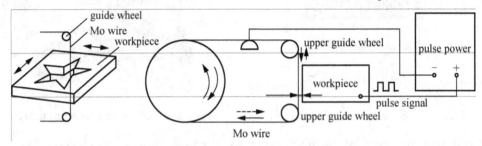

Fig. 6.14 Schematic of wire EDM process

The wires for wire EDM, which should possess high tensile strength and good electrical conductivity, is made of brass, copper, tungsten, molybdenum. Zinc or brass coated wires are also used extensively.

molybdenum 钼

3. Electrochemical Machining (ECM)

ECM is a metal-removal process based on the principle of reverse electroplating (Fig.6.15). Particles travel from the workpiece-anode toward the machining tool-cathode. A current of electrolyte fluid carries away the depleted material before it has a chance to reach the machining tool.[4] The cavity produced is the female mating image of the tool shape.

电化学加工
reverse 相反的
electroplating 电镀
electrolyte 电解
deplete 耗尽，使衰竭

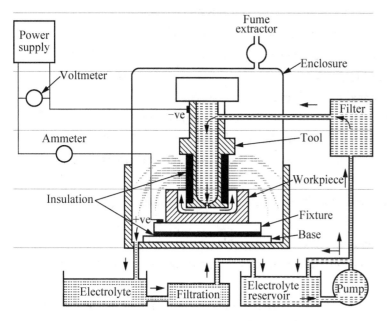

Fig. 6.15 Schematic of ECM process

fume extractor 抽烟器
enclosure 排烟罩
filter 过滤器
fixture 夹具
pump 泵
electrolyte reservoir 电解池
filtration 过滤
insulation 绝缘
voltmeter 电压表
ammeter 电流表

ECM's applications are electrochemical deburring, arc machining, grinding, hole drilling, full-form shaping, etc..

deburring 修边，去毛刺

4. Ultrasonic Machining (USM)

超声加工

USM (Fig. 6.16) is mechanical material removal process or an abrasive process used to erode holes or cavities on hard or brittle workpiece by using shaped tools, high frequency mechanical motion and an abrasive slurry.[5] USM can machine brittle materials such as single crystals, glasses and polycrystalline ceramics, and increasing complex operations to provide intricate shapes and workpiece profiles. The hard particles in slurry are accelerated toward the surface of the workpiece by a tool oscillating at a frequency up to 100 kHz. Through repeated abrasions, the tool machines a cavity of a cross section identical to its own.

abrasive 研磨的
erode 浸蚀，腐蚀
slurry 泥浆，浆
crystal 晶体
polycrystalline 多晶的
ceramics 陶瓷
intricate 复杂的
profile 轮廓，外形
oscillate 振动，振荡

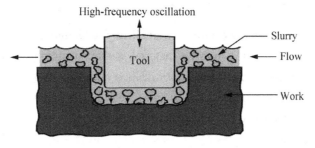

Fig. 6.16 Schematic of USM process

USM process is a non-thermal, non-chemical, creates no changes in the microstructures, chemical or physical properties of the workpiece and offers virtually stress free machined surfaces.

5. Laser–Beam Machining (LBM)

LBM (Fig. 6.17) is a thermal material-removal process that utilizes a high-energy, coherent light beam to melt and vaporize particles on the surface of metallic and non-metallic workpieces.[6] Lasers can be used to cut, drill, weld and mark. LBM is particularly suitable for making accurately placed holes.

Different types of lasers are available for manufacturing operations which are as follows.

(1) CO_2 (pulsed or continuous wave): It is a gas laser that emits light in the infrared region. It can provide up to 25 kW in continuous-wave mode.

(2) Nd-YAG: Neodymium-doped Yttrium-Aluminium-Garnet ($Y_3Al_5O_{12}$) laser is a solid-state laser which can deliver light through a fibre-optic cable. It can provide up to 50 kW power in pulsed mode and 1 kW in continuous- wave mode.

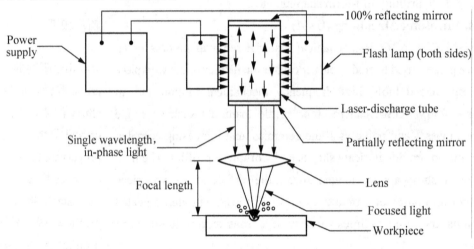

Fig. 6.17　Schematic of LBM process

LBM can make very accurate holes as small as 0.005 mm in refractory metals ceramics, and composite material without warping the workpieces. This process is used widely for drilling and cutting of metallic and non-metallic materials. Laser beam machining is being used extensively in the electronic and automotive industries.

6. Water Jet Cutting

Water jet (Fig. 6.18) technology uses the principle of pressurizing water to extremely high pressures, and allowing the water to escape through a very small opening called "orifice" or "jewel". Water jet cutting uses the beam of water exiting the orifice to cut soft materials. This method is not suitable for cutting hard materials. The inlet water is typically pressurized between 1300 ~4000 bars. This high pressure is forced through a tiny hole in the jewel, which is typically 0.18~0.4 mm in diameter.

Water jet cutting can reduce the costs and speed up the processes by eliminating or reducing expensive secondary machining process. Since no heat is applied on the materials, cut edges are clean with minimal burr. Problems such as cracked edge defects, crystallization, hardening, reduced wealdability and machinability are reduced in this process.

Water jet cutting is mostly used to cut lower strength materials such as wood, plastics and aluminum. When abrasives are added (abrasive water jet cutting, as shown in Fig. 6.19), stronger materials such as steel and tool steel can be cut.

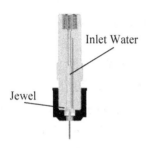

Fig. 6.18 Schematic of water jet machining

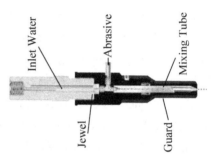

Fig. 6.19 Schematic of abrasive water jet machining

7. Abrasive Water Jet Cutting

Abrasive water jet cutting is an extended version of water jet cutting; in which the water jet contains abrasive particles such as silicon carbide or aluminum oxide in order to increase the material removal rate above that of water jet machining. Almost any type of material ranging from hard brittle materials such as ceramics, metals and glass to extremely soft materials such as foam and rubbers can be cut by abrasive water jet cutting. The narrow cutting stream and computer controlled movement enables this process to produce parts accurately and efficiently. This machining process is especially ideal for cutting materials that cannot be cut by laser or thermal cut. Metallic, non-metallic and advanced composite materials of various thicknesses can be cut by this process. This process is particularly suitable for heat sensitive materials that cannot be machined by processes that produce heat while machining.

Abrasive water jet cutting is highly used in aerospace, automotive and electronics industries. In aerospace industries, parts such as titanium bodies for military aircrafts, engine components (aluminum, titanium, heat resistant alloys), aluminum body parts and interior cabin parts are made using abrasive water jet cutting. In automotive industries, parts like interior trim (head liners, trunk liners, door panels) and fiber glass body components and bumpers are made by this process. Similarly, in electronics industries, circuit boards and cable stripping are made by abrasive water jet cutting.

titanium 钛
military 军事的
engine 发动机
cabin 舱
trim 装饰
panel 面板
liner 衬里，垫板
bumper 缓冲器
stripping 抽锭，脱芯

Notes

1. Non-traditional manufacturing processes are defined as a group of processes that remove excess material by various techniques involving mechanical, thermal, electrical or chemical energy or combinations of these energies but do not use sharp cutting tools as it needs to be used for traditional manufacturing processes.

特种加工方法是一组采用多种技术去除多余材料的加工方法，这种方法将用到机械能、热能、电能、化学能或这些能量的组合，而不会用到在传统加工工艺中所用的锋利切削刀具。

本句主句是 Non-traditional manufacturing processes are defined as a group of processes，其后是由 that 引导的定语从句，说明是一组什么样的加工方法。在 that 引导的定语从句中，有两个由 but 连接的谓语动词 remove excess material 和 do not use sharp cutting tools；by various techniques involving mechanical, thermal, ...these energies 是 remove excess material 的方式状语，as it needs to be used for traditional manufacturing processes 是 sharp cutting tools 的定语从句，说明锋利的切削刀具在传统加工方法中是需要的。

2. EDM utilizes thermoelectric process to erode undesired materials from the workpiece by a series of discrete electrical sparks between the workpiece and the electrode.

电火花加工(EDM)运用热电的方法，通过在工件和电极间产生的大量不连续的电火花侵蚀工件上多余的材料。

3. The wire EDM process can cut intricate components for the electric and aerospace industries, pattern tool steel for die manufacturing, cut cylindrical objects with high precision.

采用线切割方法能为电子和航空航天工业切割复杂的零件，为模具制造业成型钢质工具，能以很高的精度切割圆柱形零件。

4. A current of electrolyte fluid carries away the depleted material before it has a chance to reach the machining tool.

电解液的流动可以使被侵蚀掉的材料在到达机床刀具(电极)之前被冲刷走。

5. USM is mechanical material removal process or an abrasive process used to erode holes or cavities on hard or brittle workpiece by using shaped tools, high frequency mechanical motion and an abrasive slurry.

超声加工是一种机械去除材料的方法，或称其为一种研磨方法。超声加工方法利用成型刀具、高频机械运动和研磨泥在又硬又脆的工件上侵蚀出孔洞或型腔。

6. LBM is a thermal material-removal process that utilizes a high-energy, coherent light beam to melt and vaporize particles on the surface of metallic and non-metallic workpieces.

激光加工是一种利用热量去除材料的方法，它使用高能量的连续光束熔化金属或非金属工件表面的粒子，并将这些粒子汽化。

本句主句是 LBM is a thermal material-removal process，其后是由 that 引导的定语从句，说明是一种什么样的去除材料方法。在 that 引导的定语从句中，utilizes 是谓语动词，to melt and vaporize particles 是不定式短语作结果状语，on the surface of metallic and non-metallic workpieces 是介词短语作 particles 的后置定语。

 New Words and Expressions

non-traditional [ˌnɔntrəˈdiʃənəl] *adj.* 特种的
excess [ikˈses] *adj. & n.* 多余，过度，超额
combination [ˌkɔmbiˈneiʃən] *n.* 联合，合并
feasible [ˈfi:zəbl] *adj.* 可行的，切实可行的
flexible [ˈfleksəbl] *adj.* 柔软的，灵活的
slender [ˈslendə] *adj.* 薄弱的，苗条的，微弱的
utilize [ˈju:tilaiz] *v.* 利用，使用
discrete [disˈkri:t] *adj.* 不连续的，离散的
spark [spɑ:k] *n.* 瞬间放电，火花 *v.* 鼓舞，闪烁
electrode [iˈlektrəud] *n.* 电极
dominating [ˈdɔmineitiŋ] *adj.* 主要的，独裁的
schematic [skiˈmætik] *n.* 示意图 *adj.* 示意性的
immerse [iˈmə:s] *v.* 沉浸，陷入
extrusion die [eksˈtru:ʒən dai] 挤出模
discharge [disˈtʃɑ:dʒ] *n. & v.* 放电，卸货，流出
current [ˈkʌrənt] *n.* 电(水、气)流 *adj.* 流通的
capacitor [kəˈpæsitə] *n.* 电容，电容器
cathode [ˈkæθəud] *n.* 阴极，负极
anode [ˈænəud] *n.* 阳极，正极
insulating [ˈinsjuleitiŋ] *adj.* 绝缘的

voltmeter [ˈvəultˌmi:tə(r)] *n.* 电压表
ammeter [ˈæmitə] *n.* 电流表
deburring [diˈbə:riŋ] *n.* 修边，去毛刺
abrasive [əˈbreisiv] *adj.* 研磨的，粗糙的
erode [iˈrəud] *v.* 浸蚀，腐蚀，逐渐消失掉
slurry [ˈslə:ri] *n.* 泥浆，浆，粘土
crystal [ˈkristl] *n.* 晶体，结晶，水晶 *adj.* 结晶状的
polycrystalline [ˌpɔliˈkristəlain] *adj.* 多晶的
ceramics [siˈræmiks] *n.* 陶瓷
profile [ˈprəufail] *n.* 轮廓，外形，剖面，侧面
oscillate [ˈɔsileit] *v.* 振动，振荡
virtually [ˈvə:tjuəli] *adv.* 实质上，事实上
coherent [kəuˈhiərənt] *adj.* 连贯的，一致的
vaporize [ˈveipəraiz] *v.*(使)蒸发，汽化
mark [mɑ:k] *v.* 作标记 *n.* 标志，记号，分数
emit [iˈmit] *v.* 发出，放射，吐露，发表，发行
infrared [ˈinfrəˈred] *n. & adj.* 红外线
Nd-YAG 钇铝石榴石

insulation [ˌinsjuˈleiʃən] n. 绝缘(体)，隔离
dielectric [ˌdaiiˈlektrik] n. 电介质，绝缘体
suspend [səsˈpend] v. 悬挂，吊，延缓
transient [ˈtrænziənt] adj. 瞬时的，暂时的
hydrocarbon [ˈhaidrəuˈkɑːbən] n. 烃，碳氢化合物
kerosene [ˈkerəsiːn] n. 煤油，火油
deionizer [diːˈaiəˌnaiz] n. 脱离子剂
ionize [ˈaiənaiz] v. 使离子化，电离
flush [flʌʃ] v. 冲洗，淹没，脸变红
tungsten [ˈtʌŋstən] n. 钨
graphite [ˈgræfait] n. 石墨
die-sinking machine 加工凹模的机床
prescribe [prisˈkraib] v. 指示，指定，开处方
intricate [ˈintrikit] adj. 复杂的，难以理解的
aerospace [ˈɛərəuspeis] n. 航空航天
cylindrical [siˈlindrik(ə)l] adj. 圆柱体的
precision [priˈsiʒən] n. 准确，精确，精度
molybdenum [məˈlibdinəm] n. 钼
reverse [riˈvəːs] n. & adj. 相反，背面 v. 颠转
electroplating [iˈlektrəuˌpleitiŋ] n. 电镀
electrolyte [iˈlektrəulait] n. 电解，电解液
electrolyte reservoir [ˈrezəvwɑː] n. 电解池
deplete [diˈpliːt] v. 耗尽，使衰竭
fume extractor [fjuːm iksˈtræktə] n. 抽烟器
enclosure [inˈkləuʒə] n. 排烟罩
filter [ˈfiltə] n. 过滤器 v. 过滤，渗入，走漏
filtration [filˈtreiʃən] n. 过滤，筛选
fixture [ˈfikstʃə] n. 夹具，固定设备(时间)
pump [pʌmp] n. 泵，抽水机
refractory [riˈfræktəri] adj. 难溶的，难控制的
warp [wɔːp] v. 弄歪，使翘曲 n. 弯曲，偏见

fibre-optic [ˈfaibə ˈɔptik] adj. 纤维光学的
extremely [iksˈtriːmli] adv. 非常，极端地
orifice [ˈɔrifis] n. 孔，口
jewel [ˈdʒuːəl] n. 钻石瓦(轴承)，宝石，钻石
inlet [ˈinlet] n. 进口，入口，小港
tiny [ˈtaini] adj. 微小的
eliminate [iˈlimineit] v. 消除，去除
defect [diˈfekt] n. 缺点，毛病
silicon carbide [ˈsilikən ˈkɑːbaid] 金刚砂
aluminum oxide [əˈljuːminəm ˈɔksaid] 氧化铝
foam [fəum] n. 泡沫塑料 v. 使起泡沫，吐白沫
accurately [ˈækjuritli] adv. 精确地，正确地
efficiently [iˈfiʃəntli] adv. 有效地，有效率的
heat sensitive [hiːt ˈsensitiv] adj. 热敏感的
titanium [taiˈteinjəm] n. 钛
military [ˈmilitəri] adj. 军事的，军用的
engine [ˈendʒin] n. 发动机，机车，火车头
trim [trim] n. 装潢，装饰 adj. 整齐的 v. 整理，修饰
cabin [ˈkæbin] n. 舱，小屋，工作间
liner [ˈlainə] n. 衬里，垫板
panel [ˈpænl] n. 面板
bumper [ˈbʌmpə] n. 缓冲器
stripping [ˈstripiŋ] n. 抽锭，脱芯
Wire EDM 线切割
ECM 电化学加工
USM 超声加工
LBM 激光加工
Water Jet Cutting 水射流切割
Abrasive WaterJet Cutting 磨料水射流切割

Exercises

Translate the following sentences into Chinese.

As in the case of ECM, EDM is a copying process where there is no contact between tool and work. Contrary to ECM, however, there is some erosion of the tool I EDM, which must be allowed for in the tool designed to ensure accuracy of machining. A further difference arises from the fact that in EDM there is no fixed tool feed, but the gap size must be maintained in accordance with the rate of the conditions existing within the gap.

Project 7

Life and Failure of Die

Task 7.1 Life and Failure of Die

Proper selection of the die material and of the die manufacturing technique determines, to a large extent, the useful life of forming dies. Dies may have to be replaced for a number of reasons, such as changes in dimensions due to wear or plastic deformation, deterioration of the surface finish, breakdown of lubrication, and cracking or breakage.[1] In hot impression die forging, the principal modes of die failure are erosion, thermal fatigue, mechanical fatigue and permanent plastic deformation.

In erosion, also commonly called die wear, material is actually removed from the die surface by pressure and sliding of the deforming material, wear resistance of the die material, die surface temperature, relative sliding speed at the die and material interface and the nature of the interface layer are the most significant factors influencing abrasive die wear.

Thermal fatigue occurs on the surface of the die impression in hot forming and results in "heat checking". Thermal fatigue results from cyclic yielding of the die surface due to contact with the hot deforming material. This contact cause the surface layers to expand, and, because of the very steep temperature gradients, the surface layers are subject to compressive stresses. At sufficiently high temperatures, these compressive stresses may cause the surface layers to deform. When the die surface cools, a stress reversal may occur and the surface layers will then be in tension. After repeated cycling in this manner, fatigue will cause formation of a crack pattern that is recognized

extent 程度，范围

deterioration 变坏,退化
breakdown 崩溃，击穿
lubrication 润滑
cracking 裂化，开裂
breakage 破坏，断裂
erosion 腐蚀，侵蚀
fatigue 疲劳
permanent 永久的
influence 影响，感化

abrasive 研磨的

checking 微裂，龟裂
cyclic 循环的，轮转的
yielding 变形，屈服
expand 膨胀
compressive 压缩的
steep 急剧升降的
gradient 梯度，倾斜度
reversal 撤销，逆转
tension 拉伸

as heat checking.

Die breakage or cracking is due to mechanical fatigue and occurs in cases where the dies are overloaded and local stresses are high.² The dies are subjected to alternating stresses due to loading and unloading during the deformation process, and this cause crack initiation and eventual failure.

Die life and die failure are greatly affected by the mechanical properties of the die materials under the conditions that exist in a given deformation process.³ Generally, the properties that are most significant depend on the process temperature. Thus, die materials used in cold forming processes are quite different from those used in hot forming.

The design and manufacturing of dies and the selection of die materials are very important in the production of discrete parts by use of metal forming processes. The dies must be made by modern manufacturing methods from appropriate die material in order to provide acceptable die life at a reasonable cost. Often the economic success of a forming process depends on die life and die costs per piece produced. For a given application, selection of the appropriate die material depends on three types of variables.

(1) Variable related to the process itself, including factors such as size of the die cavity, type of machine used, deformation speed, initial stock size, temperature to be used, lubrication, production rate and number of parts to be produced.⁴

(2) Variable related to the type of die loading, including speed of loading, i.e., impact or gradual contact time between dies and deforming metal (this contact time is especially important in hot forming), maximum load and pressure on the dies, maximum and minimum die temperatures, and number of loading cycles to which the dies will be subjected.

(3) Mechanical properties of the die material, including hardenability, impact strength, hot strength (if hot forming is considered) and resistance to thermal and mechanical fatigue.

 Notes

1. Dies may have to be replaced for a number of reasons, such as changes in dimensions due to wear or plastic deformation, deterioration of the surface finish, breakdown of lubrication, and cracking or breakage.

更换模具有很多原因，例如，由于磨损或塑性变形造成尺寸变化，成型表面腐蚀退化，润滑油作用损坏，以及开裂和细纹损坏。

2. Die breakage or cracking is due to mechanical fatigue and occurs in cases where the dies are overloaded and local stresses are high.

模具的开裂和细纹损坏是由于机械疲劳造成的，这种开裂和细纹损坏发生在模具过载和局部应力过高的情况下。

is due to 和 occurs 是 Die breakage or cracking 的两个谓语动词。

where the dies are overloaded and local stresses are high 是 cases 的定语从句。

3. Die life and die failure are greatly affected by the mechanical properties of the die materials under the conditions that exist in a given deformation process.

模具的使用寿命和模具的失效在极大程度上要受到模具材料在已给定的成型加工工艺条件下所表现出的机械性能的影响。

that exist in a given deformation process 是 conditions 的定语从句。

4. Variable related to the process itself, including factors such as size of the die cavity, type of machine used, deformation speed, initial stock size, temperature to be used, lubrication, production rate and number of parts to be produced.

与工艺本身相关的变量包括模具型腔的尺寸、所采用的机床型号、变形速度、毛坯的初始尺寸、加工时的温度、润滑条件、生产率和零件批量。

 New Words and Expressions

extent [iks'tent] n. 程度，范围，广度，区域
deterioration [di,tiəriə'reiʃən] n. 变坏，退化
breakdown ['breikdaun] n. 崩溃，击穿，分解
lubrication [,lu:bri'keiʃən] n. 润滑，润滑油
cracking ['krækiŋ] n. 裂化，开裂
breakage ['breikidʒ] n. 破坏，断裂，损坏量
erosion [i'rəuʒən] n. 腐蚀，侵蚀
fatigue [fə'ti:g] n. & v. 疲劳，疲乏
permanent ['pə:mənənt] adj. 永久的，持久的
influence ['influəns] n. & v. 影响，感化
abrasive [ə'breisiv] adj. 研磨的 n. 研磨剂
checking ['tʃekiŋ] n. 微裂，龟裂，检查，核算
cyclic ['saiklik] adj. 循环的，轮转的
yielding ['ji:ldiŋ] n. 变形，屈服 adj. 屈从的
expand [iks'pænd] v. 膨胀，扩张，发展
compressive [kəm'presiv] adj. 压缩的
steep [sti:p] adj. 急剧升降的，陡峭的 n. 悬崖

gradient ['greidiənt] n. 梯度，倾斜度 adj. 斜的
reversal [ri'və:səl] n. 撤销，逆转，反转
tension ['tenʃən] n. 拉伸，紧张，拉紧，张力
overload ['əuvə'ləud] n. & v. 过载
alternating [ɔ:l'tə:nitiŋ] adj. 交互的
initiation [i,niʃi'eiʃən] n. 开始
initial [i'niʃəl] adj. 初始的，最初的，词首的
eventual [i'ventjuəl] adj. 最后的，结果的
process [prə'ses] n. 工序，步骤 v. 加工，处理
discrete [dis'kri:t] adj. 不连续的，离散的
appropriate [ə'prəupriit] adj. 适当的
variable ['vɛəriəbl] n. 变量，变数 adj. 可变的
cavity ['kæviti] n. 型腔，洞
stock [stɔk] n. 坯料，原料，库存，股票，血统
gradual ['grædjuəl] adj. 逐渐的，逐步的
hardenability [,ha:dənə'biliti] n. 淬透性，可淬性

Exercises

I. Translate the following phrases into Chinese.

1. plastic deformation _____ 2. lubrication _____ 3. cracking or breakage _____
4. mechanical fatigue _____ 5. temperature gradient _____ 6. impact strength _____
7. alternating stress _____ 8. die cavity _____

II. Translate the following sentences into Chinese.

1. Proper selection of the die material and of the die manufacturing technique determines, to a large extent, the useful life of forming dies.

2. Mechanical properties of the die material, including hardenability, impact strength, hot strength (if hot forming is considered) and resistance to thermal and mechanical fatigue.

III. Answer the questions according to the text.

1. What are the most significant factors influencing die wear?
2. What does selection of the appropriate die material depend on for a given application?

Task 7.2 Effects of Surface Treatment and Lubricant on Die Life

The process of metal forming is always accompanied by heat generation. This heat due to plastic deformation and the friction of the interface results in a complex and changing temperature field.[1] To predict the temperature field during the forging processes is very important since it influences the lubrication conditions, the material behavior during deformation, the quality of finished parts and the service life of the die.

The service life of the die is restricted by wear, thermal cracking and fatigue, and plastic deformation, etc. There have been many research projects to investigate the influence of these factors on tool life. In general, however, the surface hardness of the die decreases when the temperature of the die increases during repeated operations, which induces thermal softening warm forging processes. The thermal softening accelerates the wear, thermal cracking and fatigue, and the plastic deformation of the die.

In order to increase the die life, heat treatments have been performed for the die to increase the surface hardness, and surface treatments are also applied to the die to reduce the friction and to increase the thermal insulation. The thermal properties of the die change due to the surface treatments.

accompany 陪伴
friction 摩擦

predict 预知，预报
lubrication 润滑

service 服务，服役
restrict 限制，约束

project 计划，设计
investigate 调查，研究

accelerate 加速，促进
cracking 开裂
fatigue 疲劳

insulation 绝缘

The roles of lubricants are to reduce friction between the die and the workpiece and to reduce heat-transfer from the billet to the die during the forming processes.[2] Graphite, a solid lubricant, is sprayed onto the die or workpiece before the warm forming process. The heat-transfer coefficient, from the billet to the die, has different values according to the kind of graphite. In addition, the selection of suitable lubricant for the extending die life leads to reduce heat-transfer from the workpiece to the die.

billet 钢坯
graphite 石墨
spray 喷射
coefficient 系数

The main factors affecting die service life are the surface treatment and the lubricants that are related to thermal softening.[3] High surface hardness and the poor heat-transfer make extending of the die life.

Notes

1. This heat due to plastic deformation and the friction of the interface results in a complex and changing temperature field.

塑性变形产生的热量和接口间的摩擦导致一个既复杂又不断变化的温度场产生。

本句有两个主语，分别是 this heat 和 the friction；due to plastic deformation 是形容词短语作 this heat 的后置定语，of the interface 是介词短语作 the friction 的后置定语。

2. The roles of lubricants are to reduce friction between the die and the workpiece and to reduce heat-transfer from the billet to the die during the forming processes.

润滑的作用在于减少在成型加工过程中模具和工件间产生的摩擦以及从钢坯向模具进行的热传递。

本句 to reduce friction 和 to reduce heat-transfer 是两个并列的不定式短语作表语。

3. The main factors affecting die service life are the surface treatment and the lubricants that are related to thermal softening.

影响模具使用寿命的主要因素是与热软化作用相关的表面热处理和润滑。

New Words and Expressions

accompany [əˈkʌmpəni] v. 陪伴，伴随，伴奏
friction [ˈfrikʃən] n. 摩擦，摩擦力
predict [priˈdikt] v. 预知，预报，预言
lubrication [ˌluːbriˈkeiʃən] n. 润滑，润滑油
service [ˈsəːvis] n. 服务，服役 v. 保养，维修
restrict [risˈtrikt] v. 限制，约束，限定
project [ˈprɔdʒekt] v. 计划，设计 n. 方案，事业
investigate [inˈvestigeit] v. 调查，研究

accelerate [ækˈseləreit] v. 加速，促进
cracking [ˈkrækiŋ] n. 裂化，开裂
fatigue [fəˈtiːg] n. & v. 疲劳，疲乏
insulation [ˌinsjuˈleiʃən] n. 绝缘
billet [ˈbilit] n. 钢坯，兵舍，工作职位
graphite [ˈgræfait] n. 石墨
spray [sprei] v. 喷射，喷溅 n. 喷雾，飞沫
coefficient [ˌkəuiˈfiʃənt] n. 系数

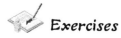 **Exercises**

I. Translate the following phrases into Chinese.

1. thermal cracking and fatigue _____ 2. thermal softening _____
3. solid lubricant _____ 4. heat-transfer _____ 5. surface treatment _____

II. Answer the questions according to the text.

1. What's the main factor influencing die life in most metal forming application? And why?

2. What are the surface treatments and lubricants used in this study for warm forging die life?

Reading Materials

NO.1 Slideways

Guideways, are made of cast iron. They are hardened to 56 Rockwell C, then precision ground. They are protected by force lubrication and wipers. The wiper consists of a scraper and a rubber wiper. This protects the guideways from large chips and fine particles.

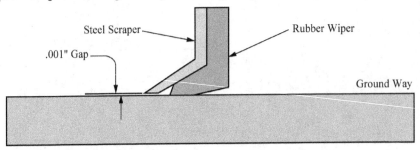

Slideways, are made of cast iron also, but are hand scraped to fit(8~10 bearing points per square inch). Scraping is done to allow good contact between slideway and guideway. This scraping creates small oil pockets to aid in lubricating the two surfaces. Some slideways are fitted with a special surface called Turkite to help in keeping the surface lubricated. As shown below, oil grooves are provided so that oil can be fed over the entire slideway surface.

There is a side discharge port that allows oil to flow smoothly, also this port prevents the saddle from lifting due to excessive oil. The location of the port is important, due to axis movement, chips can not enter in slideway.

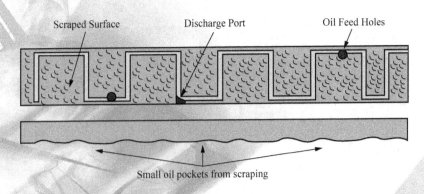

NO.2 Lubrication Distribution

Lubrication oil feed is classified into two types: the piston type and the resistance type.

(1) Piston type distribution: The piston type distributor measures and distributes oil intermittently by means of oil pressure.

① The oil allocated for the lubrication point is in front of the piston in the distributor.

② When oil is fed by the central lubrication pump, it moves the piston so that the oil in front is pushed by the main line pressure to the lubrication point.

③ On release of the main line pressure, the piston in the distributor returns to its initial position, allowing the oil to flow into the space in front of it.

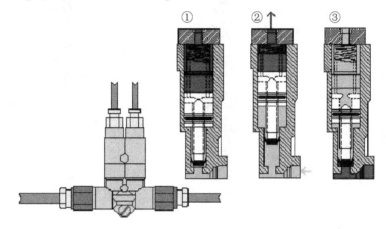

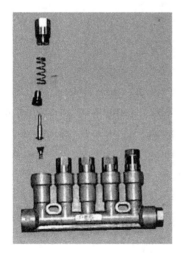

Piston type distribution

(2) Resistant type distribution: The resistant type distributor feeds oil through a resistive chamber.

The lubrication pump supplies oil to the chamber through a filter. The amount of oil is regulated by the diameter of the rod resisting the flow. The check valve is used to prevent the counterflow of lubrication so that the distributor may be installed in any orientation.

NOTE: When replacing the metering valve on either system, check the size of the valve before ordering a new one. The size is the number stamped on the side of the valve.

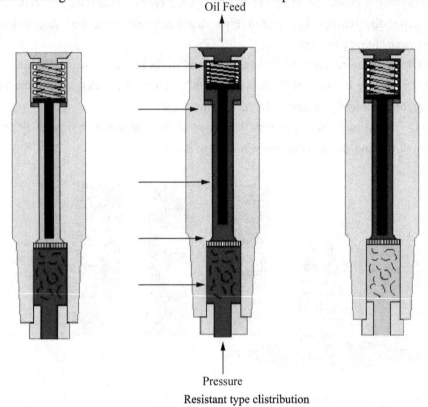

Resistant type clistribution

NO.3 Troubleshooting

Symptom: System uses excessive oil

Possible causes:

(1) Piston distributors are stuck open, which allows large amounts of oil to flow out of one or more discharge points. Solution: Trace the source excess oil back to the piston distributor which has a port stuck open and replace that piston distributor.

(2) Leaking system from a broken tube, broken or worn hose. Solution: Repair or replace component.

(3) Hole in reservoir. Solution: Replace reservoir.

(4) Timer is coming on too frequently. Solution: Adjust timer.

Symptom: System uses too little oil or no oil.

Possible causes:

(1) Pump is worn out and will not develop enough pressure. Solution: Replace the pump or lubricator.

(2) Motor is not functioning. Solution: Replace motor.

(3) Restricted or clogged filters. Solution: Replace filters.

(4) Check valve may be leaking returning oil to tank. Solution: Replace the piston distributor.

Symptom: System initiates a failure light or trouble code in its control board.

Possible causes:

(1) System is not producing enough pressure to satisfy the pressure switch. Solution: Check the pump pressure by blocking off the supply lines immediately after the pump. If the pressure goes up check for a broken line, loose fitting, or piston distributors which are stuck open. If pressure does not go up check for a clogged filter. If no clog is found, the pump is worn out and needs replacing.

(2) Pressure switch is not working. Solution: Replace pressure switch. Pressure switches can be built into the lubricators or found anywhere within the lubrication system. Float switch is not working. Solution: Replace float switch. Float switches can be changed from normally open to normally closed and vice versa by removing the clip at the bottom of the stem, flipping the float 180 degrees and reinstalling.

NO.4 Chemical Conversion Coatings on Aluminum and Aluminum Alloys

(1) Chemical conversion materials: The materials used to produce a chemical conversion coating shall be approved for the selected class, form and application method in accordance with the qualification requirements of the products and been accepted for listing on the applicable Qualified Products List. Replenishing chemicals, such as fluorides, added to a bath to maintain its efficiency, shall in no way degrade the performance of the coating being applied.

(2) Cleaning: Prior to coating, the base metal shall be mechanically and/or chemically cleaned such that a water break-free surface is obtained after rinsing. Abrasives containing iron such as steel wool, iron oxide, rouge or steel wire are prohibited for all cleaning operation as particles from them may become embedded in the metal and accelerate corrosion of the aluminum and aluminum alloys. Treated parts which have become soiled shall be cleaned with materials which will remove the soil without damaging the base metal, the part, or the conversion coating. If the coating is damaged, the damaged area shall be recleaned and recoated or the part shall be rejected.

(3) Application: Unless an application method is specified, the chemical conversion materials shall be applied nonelectrolytically by spray, brush or immersion after all the heat treatments and mechanical operations such as forming, perforating, machining, brazing and welding have been completed. Assemblies containing non-aluminum parts which may be attacked, embrittled, or damaged in any way by the conversion coating process shall not be coated as assembles unless the non-aluminum parts are suitably masked.

NO.5　Outline of the Controls

In this section, an outline of the controls on the NC operation panel and the machine operation panel is provided.

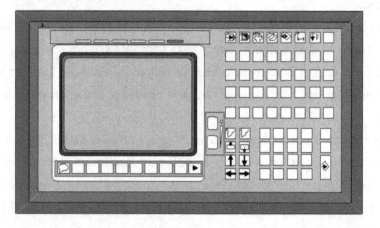

Controls on NC Operation Panel

 Manual: Press this when operating the machine manually.

 MDI (Manual Data Input): Operating the machine with the commands entered through the keyboard.

 Auto: Operating the machine in the automatic mode by the part program.

 Tool data: When setting, modifying, or checking tool offset data and tool nose radius data.

 Zero set: When setting, or modifying the reference point of the machine Reference zero), or checking the stored coordinate values of such position.

 Parameter: When setting, modifying, or checking parameters. i.e., stroke end, variable soft-limit, backlash, chuck barrier, droop, spindle jog speed, etc..

 Edit aux: When editing, or inputting/outputting the stored part program, or when checking contents of the program.

 Write: Press this key to select the operation mode or setting the data in the MDI mode.

BS: Press this when an erroneous data has been entered. When pressed, each character entered will be erased.

Cancel: Press this when an erroneous data has been entered. When pressed, each line input is erased.

Turret: Used to select A upper turret or B lower turret. These buttons are not used, when the machine only has an upper turret.

NO.6 Fundamental Machine Operation Procedure

Manual Operations: NC lathes operate in three different modes: Manual, Auto, and MDI. This section deals with manual machine operation procedure, which will provide you with the most fundamental knowledge to operate the machine.

When turning power supply to the machine ON for the first time after machine installation, **make sure** that your power supply is compatible with the machine and control. If not compatible this could cause the machine to be damaged.

1. Turning Power ON

(1) Turn the main switch on the left side of the electrical control enclosure ON. This turns 200 volt AC power to the electrical control system. The hydraulic power unit pump motor starts at the same time.

(2) Press the CONTROL ON button on the machine operation panel. This turns on the power supply to the CPU and relay circuit. After the NC software has been loaded, the NC starts to run messages on the CRT. This will allow the operator to know if there are any faulty loading processes.

After steps one and two have completed, the control becomes ready to operate and the CRT display changes to NC operation. The servo drive circuit and other control circuits are energized at the same time.

The RESET button resets the control during operation, or when an ALARM is indicated.

2. Turning Power OFF

(1) Press the CONTROL OFF button on the machine operation panel. This turns the power supply off to the CPU, servo drive system, relays, and magnetic circuits.

(2) Turn the main switch on the left side of the control enclosure OFF. This turns off the power supply to the machine.

3. Emergency Stop

To stop machine operation when some abnormal state takes place, press the EMERGENCY STOP button on the machine operation panel. This cuts off power supply to the hydraulic power unit and servo drive unit, but CPU is still active. Press the CONTROL ON button and control will return to normal state.

MDI Operations:

(1) Press MDI key in mode select area.

(2) Press function key (F3) (Program).

(3) Press Page until MDI display appears with current/buffer.

(4) Press function key (F1) (Data Input).

(5) Enter the MDI data (G00 X20 Z20 S50 T10101).

(6) Press Write key, at this point the MDI data is transferred to the buffer side of the MDI screen.

(7) Before pressing cycle start, decrease the feed rate switch to minimize rapid movements.

(8) Press Cycle/Start, at this point MDI data is transferred from Buffer to Current side of the screen and the machine executes your command.

NO.7 Hydraulic Power Units

Hydraulic pressures are preset at the factory for normal operation of the machine. NOTE, that it is very important to change the oil after the first month of operation, then every six months thereafter. When changing oil remember to clean the strainer and the tank, also check the pressures from each of the solenoid valves.

Each of the valves also have an override switch built inside of the valve. If the valve ever sticks you can use this override to move the valve spool. This helps to blow out any trash that may get into the valve.

When adjusting the pressure refer to your maintenance manual for the proper limits. To make an adjustment loosen the lock nut and set the desired pressure by turning the adjustment knob. See illustration below.

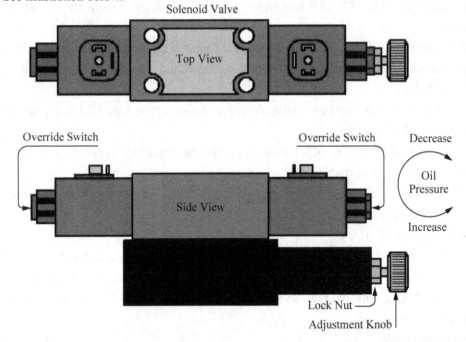

NO.8 Noise or Vibration When The Spindle Is Running

There isn't any evidence of a crash.

(1) Were any of the pulleys recently removed. If so there could be a misalignment of the pulleys. They should line up to each other within 0.2mm (.008"). Check the pulleys for nicks, dinges, or damage that would cause the belt to not seat properly.

(2) Check the belts for nicks or any chips imbedded in them.

(3) Check the runout on the hydraulic cylinder. The runout on the end of the cylinder should not be greater than 0.03mm (.0012"). This runout will cause the most noise or vibration at about 1800 RPM or at 3000 RPM.

Check the spindle nose for runout. Set the indicator on the OD taper of the spindle at a right angle. Mount the indicator on a solid base, such as on the slideway, or bed, not on a cover. Run the spindle at 50 RPM and take the maximum difference. The tolerance is 0.01mm (.0004").

Check the spindle for axial slip. Set the indicator against the face of the spindle and at a right angle. Take the maximum difference with the spindle running at 50 RPM. The tolerance is 0.015mm (.0006").

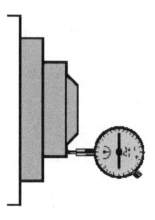

(4) Using a Brass part 4" in diameter, face it using the following Parameters: CSS- 1000 Ft./

min, feedrate- .002", depth of cut- .002".

Face from the outside to the center.

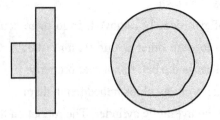

If the finish shows a non-circular polygon mark on the face, the most likely cause is the spindle motor or spindle bearings. Check the tooling, program, and chuck first.

NO.9 Case Study: Ropes

1. Ranking Candidate Materials

To satisfy the design requirements for suspension cables, we need:

high modulus and strength, plus low weight, therefore we look at specific(i.e. divided by density) properties.

2. Climbing Ropes

Elastic strain at failure=strength/Young's modulus

Elastic energy stored at failure(per unit volume)=1/2 × strength × Elastic strain at failure.

Use the data to calculate these quantities, and see if the materials used for climbing ropes have good values of failure strain and stored energy at failure.

Extra:Using the data in the table, convert the figures you have calculated for stored energy per unit volume into stored energy per unit mass. When might this be a more useful property to use in selecting a material?

3. Safety Factors in Design

(1) For parachute lines and climing ropes, where safety is the most important requirement, designers apply what is called a "safety factor".

(2) If you design a product that has to be strong and design it to survive to 5 times the expected maximum load, this is a safety factor of 5.

(3) Thanks of as many applications as you can of ropes, cables or wires which are designed to carry tensile loads.

(4) Which products would you design with the highest safety factors, and why?

NO.10 模具类企业常用词汇

stamping, press 冲压

die casting dies 压铸冲模

die casting machines 压铸机

dies-progressive 连续冲模

gravity casting machines 重力铸造机

foundry equipment 铸造设备

forging dies 锻模
forging,aluminium 锻铝
forging,cold 冷锻
forging,copper 铜锻
forging,other 其他锻造
forging,steel 钢锻
jigs 钻模
punch press, dieing out press 冲床
uncoiler & strainghtener 整平机
feeder 送料机
rack, shelf, stack 料架
cylinder 油缸
to take apart a die 卸下模具
to load a die 装上模具
to tight a bolt 拧紧螺栓
to looser a bolt 拧松螺栓
to move away a die plate 移走模板
easily damaged parts 易损件
standard parts 标准件
breaking, (be)broken, (be)cracked 断裂
compression molding 压缩成型
flash mold 溢流式模具
plsitive mold 挤压式模具
split mold 分割式模具
cavity 型控母模
core 模心公模
taper 锥拔
leather cloak 仿皮革
shiver 饰纹
flow mark 流痕
welding mark 溶合痕
post screw insert 螺纹套筒埋值
self tapping screw 自攻螺丝
striper plate 脱料板
piston 活塞
cylinder 汽缸套
chip 细碎物
handle mold 手持式模具
encapsulation molding 低压封装成型、射出成型用模具

two plate 两极式(模具)
well type 蓄料井
insulated runner 绝缘浇道方式
hot runner 热浇道
runner plat 浇道模块
valve gate 阀门浇口
band heater 环带状的电热器
spindle 阀针
spear head 刨尖头
slag well 冷料井
cold slag 冷料渣
air vent 排气道
welding line 熔合痕
eject pin 顶出针
knock pin 顶出销
return pin 回位销反顶针
sleave 套筒
stripper plate 脱料板
runner stripper plate 浇道脱料板
guide pin 导销
eject rod (bar)(成型机)顶业捧
subzero 深冷处理
three plate 三极式模具
runner system 浇道系统
stress crack 应力电裂
orientation 定向
sprue gate 射料浇口，直浇口
nozzle 射嘴
sprue lock pin 料头钩销(拉料杆)
slag well 冷料井
side gate 侧浇口
edge gate 侧缘浇口
tab gate 搭接浇口
film gate 薄膜浇口
slit gate 缝隙浇口
fan gate 扇形浇口
dish gate 因盘形浇口
diaphragm gate 隔膜浇口
ring gate 环形浇口

subarine gate 潜入式浇口
tunnel gate 隧道式浇口
pin gate 针点浇口
runner less 无浇道
sprue less 无射料管方式
long nozzle 延长喷嘴方式
mold & die components 模具单元
mold changing systems 换模系统
mold core 模芯
mold heaters/chillers 模具加热器/冷却器
mold polishing/texturing 模具打磨/磨纹
mold repair 模具维修

参 考 译 文

项目1 机械基础

1.1 工程制图

工程制图是向人们表达设计师意图的一种抽象的通用语言，它是在工业和工程中的各个方面使用最普遍的沟通媒介。

在现代制造工业中，制图的标准类型是多视图(如图1.1所示)。多视图通常包含两个或3个视图(主视图、俯视图和左视图)。每个视图都是一个平面的正交投影。在美国和加拿大使用第三角视图(如图1.2所示)。

1. 坐标系

笛卡儿坐标系是AutoCAD中所有输入的基础，不同的输入方法(绝对坐标值或相对坐标值)都依赖于这个系统。另外，AutoCAD中有两个内部坐标系可以用来在绘图区中进行定位：全局坐标系和用户坐标系。固定的笛卡儿坐标系是通过定义一系列用以确定空间位置的正负轴来定位AutoCAD图中的所有点的。

2. 视图种类

工程制图有许多视图类型：投影视图、辅助视图、全视图、细节放大视图、旋转视图、半视图、剖视图、爆炸视图、局部视图等。

3. 配合

两个装配零件间的配合是一种由装配时所产生的间隙或过盈而引发的关系。有3种配合形式，即间隙、过渡和过盈。

4. 互换性

可互换的零件是一种能由同一图纸加工出来的相似零件所替代的零件。零件的互换性要基于两个功能。

① 对相互匹配的零件来说，设计成同一尺寸极限是十分必要的。

② 必须在指定的公差内制造零件。

5. 尺寸极限(尺寸公差)

在对一个具体尺寸指定公差带时，有3个要考虑的因素：功能重要性、互换性和经济性。为了帮助设计者选择极限与配合以及鼓励整个工业界的统一，已经有许多关于极限与配合的体系被发布了。

1.2 材料的种类和特性

主要的工具材料可分为三大类：钢铁材料、非钢铁材料与非金属材料。钢铁工具材料以铁作为基体，包括工具钢、碳钢、合金钢和铸铁。非铁金属材料则不以铁作为基体，包括铝、镁、锌、铅、铋、铜以及各种合金。非金属材料不含金属基体，包括木头、塑料、橡胶、环氧树脂、陶瓷和金刚石。

为了恰当地选择材料，必须掌握材料的一些物理性能和机械性能，以便确定所选的材料对功能和操作有何影响。

物理性能和机械性能是控制材料在特定状况下如何变化的特性。物理性能是材料固有的属性，如果不改变材料本身，这些性能永远都不会发生变化。物理性能包括质量、颜色、导热性与导电性、热膨胀率和熔点。机械性能是指材料在热加工或机械加工情况下被永久改变的性能。机械性能包括强度、硬度、耐磨性、韧性、脆性、塑性、柔软性、延展性、可锻性和弹性模量。

在多数应用场合中，不只一种材料能够满足要求，一般根据材料的可利用性和经济因素做出合理选择。

根据各种加工方法的加工参数、产品零件的生产周期和数量，模具必须满足各种各样的要求。因此，模具可由多种材料制成，包括像纸张、石膏这样的奇异材料，也就不奇怪了。但是由于大多数加工需要很高的压力和温度，金属仍然是目前最重要的材料，而钢铁则是金属中的首选。有趣的是，在许多情况下，选择模具材料不仅要考虑材料的性能和最佳的性价比，还要考虑模具的制造方法，因而整体设计会受到这些因素的影响。

1.3 钢

人类使用的金属材料90%以上的成分是铁合金。钢铁是工程材料中的一个巨大家族，它们的微观结构差别很大，并且是有相互关联的特性。多数要求结构有一定的承载力或传输动力的工程设计都会涉及到铁合金。实际上，合金根据其成分中的碳含量分为两大类：含碳量在0.05%～2.0%之间的一般称为钢，含碳量在2.0%～4.5%之间的一般称为铸铁。

钢分为两大类：碳素钢和合金钢。

1. 碳钢

碳钢是指那些仅仅由铁和碳以及少量的其他合金元素构成的钢。随着碳钢中含碳量的增加，金属经过热处理后强度、韧性和硬度也会有所增加。碳钢是一种最常见、最廉价的用于制造工具的钢。

(1) 低碳钢含碳量大约为0.05%～0.25%，是易被机械加工和焊接的软、韧钢。由于含碳量低，除了通过表面淬火进行硬化处理，无法将这些钢硬化。低碳钢适合用在以下应用中：刀具体、手柄、模座以及类似的没有强度和耐磨性要求的应用。

(2) 中碳钢含碳量大约为0.25%～0.6%，应用于对强度和韧性要求较高的部件。由于中碳钢中含碳量较高，所以经过热处理后可被制成如圆柱头螺栓、销、轴和螺母之类的部件。中碳钢比低碳钢贵，也比低碳钢难于进行机械加工和焊接。

(3) 高碳钢含碳量大约为 0.6%～1.5%，是最容易硬化的一种碳钢，常用于制作对耐磨性要求非常高的部件。适合用高碳钢制作的其他部件包括衬套、定位销和耐磨垫板。由于这些钢的碳含量很高，所以用高碳钢制成的部件通常难以进行机械加工和焊接。

2. 合金钢

合金钢是指包含其他合金元素，如铬、镍、锰、钒、钼、钨等的碳钢。添加的合金元素可以使钢的性能得到必要的改善，例如提高强度，增加耐蚀性。然而，由于合金元素总是增加材料成本，所以合金钢不能被广泛应用于大多数工具中。低合金钢和高合金刚之间一共可以增加 5%的非碳成分。

(1) 低合金钢材由于所含合金不多所以价格适中，且具有足够的韧性，易于成型，产品坚固耐用。如球轴承材料的应用、汽车车身金属板的组成等。一类有趣的合金钢——高强度低合金钢是为了满足降低汽车重量的要求而产生的。许多商业低合金高强度钢的成分是专有的，且根据其机械性能来指定。低合金高强度的钢是通过选定最佳的成分及进行精确的工艺控制如热轧得到的。

(2) 不锈钢和工具钢是两种常用的高合金钢。不锈钢是指高铬钢和高镍-铬钢。铬含量至少为 4%，通常高于 10%，这些钢常用于耐高温和耐腐蚀性空气的场合。一些高铬钢能够通过热处理硬化，应用于要求耐磨损、耐腐蚀的场合。不锈钢的典型应用就是塑料注塑模具，因为高的含铬量使得这种钢材可以被高度抛光并且能防止由于高温和腐蚀造成的型腔磨损。工具钢常用于切削、成形加工或其他材料的压力加工。工具钢中的主要合金元素有钨、铬和钼。它们的优点是能够通过简单的热处理得到所需的硬度并且能够在高温加工时保持其硬度。

1.4　铸　　铁

根据前面所讲的内容，本书将铸铁定义为含碳量大于2%的合金，铸铁一般也包含高达3%的硅用来控制石墨化的倾向。铸铁相对来讲熔点低、流动性好，浇注后易形成所需的表面，在凝固和冷却过程中收缩率适中。铸铁必须在复杂形状的良好成型性和与可锻金属相比较差的力学性能之间找到一个平衡点。

将熔融状态的铸铁浇注到模具中可形成零件的最终形状。模具的形状与凝固后金属的形状一致。由于微观结构不均匀，包括有些气孔，这些都使得铸铁的机械性能比较差。锻造合金的铸造，只要符合近似的形状即可，形状相对简单。

铸铁一般分为 4 种类型。白口铸铁的特点是断口表面呈白色。铸造后形成大量渗碳体，使得材料性能硬脆。灰铸铁具有一种多片状石墨的精细结构灰色断裂面。硅的质量百分比达到2%～3%时，可显著促进石墨的析出，抑制渗碳体(Fe_3C)的形成。必须指出的是石墨薄片有助于灰铸铁产生脆性。通过增加少量(质量占 5%)的镁到灰铸铁的熔融金属中，就可以析出球状石墨而不是片状。延展性增加了 20 倍，而强度增加了 1 倍。可锻铸铁是一种更传统的、具有较好韧性的铸铁。它最初被浇注成白口铸铁，然后通过热处理析出小球状的石墨。

1.5 聚 合 物

聚合物是由许多长链分子组成的化合物，这些长链分子又是由若干个重复的单元(链节)构成的。金属、陶瓷、玻璃都是无机材料，这里讨论的聚合物是有机材料。聚合物这个词是 1832 年由瑞典化学家 Jims Berzelius 从希腊语里创造出来的：poly 意思是"很多"，mer 意思是"部分"。聚合物也被称为"高分子"或"巨大分子"，"巨大分子"这个词是在 1922 年由德国化学家 Hermann Staudinger 提出的。

作为重要的材料，聚合物广泛地应用于不同的商业形式：光纤、薄膜和薄片、泡沫和块状泡沫。"塑料"是聚合物的一个普通的同义词，这个名字源于与多数聚合物产品的制造过程紧密联系的可塑性。然而现今，塑料被认为就是由合成树脂制造而成的各种产品。合成树脂可以采用各种化学过程制成。

聚合作用是一个由许多相对较小的有机分子形成长链分子或网状分子的过程。与无机材料相比聚合物的结构特点是相当独特的。通常，聚合物的熔点和硬度会随着聚合程度以及分子结构的复杂程度的增大而增长。

聚合物或塑料主要分为两种类型：热固性塑料和热塑性塑料。经过初步的加热，热固性塑料软化和熔解，熔料在压力作用下充满模具型腔。当继续加热时，热固性塑料发生聚合，即发生化学变化，这使得热固性塑料发硬至永久硬化、很难熔化及很难溶解的状态。热固性塑料制件成型后，再加热也不能熔融和软化。热塑性塑料受热软化、熔融，冷却后就固化定型。可以反复地对其进行加热和冷却，却能保持化学特性不发生变化。

在塑料中加入的其他材料称为填充剂。填充剂可用来增加体积、改善塑料的性能。含有填充物的塑料凝固得更快，并且能更加接近已制定的尺寸，原因在于填充物可使塑料的收缩率下降。其中最通用的填充剂是木粉。由棉绒纤维制成的棉绒填料可增加塑料的力学性能，将棉绒纤维切成 0.5in^2 截面，加入塑料中可以增强塑料的强度和抗冲击性能。用石棉纤维作为填料可增强塑料的耐热性和耐火性，而用云母可使塑料具有良好的电绝缘性能。玻璃纤维、硅、纤维素、粘土或硬壳粉同样可作为填充剂使用。硬壳粉常常用于替代木屑粉，以得到更好的表面精度。用短纤维填料能降低塑料成本，而使用长纤维可使塑料性能增强，但价格较贵。除了填料外，也可加入染料、颜料、润滑剂、加速剂和增塑剂等其他材料。加入增塑剂可增加塑料的柔韧性，改善其流动性。通常在塑料原料充模成型之前加入填料和修饰剂等材料。

化学家和化学工程师已经发现和研制了大量的塑料。目前在有机化学方面，人造树脂的研究是最为突出的领域之一。

1.6 钢的热处理

热处理在现代机械工程中的作用不容小觑，其目的是通过加热金属或合金到一定的温度，然后以各种速度冷却去改变其组织结构来控制金属或合金的性能。将加热和可控制的冷却处理相结合，不仅可以决定微观组织的性质和分布，还可以决定晶粒的大小。其中，微观组织的性质和分布又可以决定材料的性能。通过热处理使得金属性质发生变化是非常重要的。

热处理状态的特性参数有加热温度、在此温度下的保温时间、加热速度和冷却速度。一般来说，冷却速度是主要因素，超过临界速度范围的迅速冷却将导致外表面产生硬皮，非常缓慢的冷却会产生相反的结果。含铁材料的热处理包含几个重要操作，常常被冠以各种名称，例如正火、退火、淬火、回火、表面硬化、球化和消除应力。

退火的主要目的是使硬度较高的钢变软，以利于进行机械加工或冷加工。通常的操作是把钢稍微加热到临界温度以上形成奥氏体并保温，当整个零件的温度完全均衡后再慢慢地冷却，以保证零件表面与中心的温度大致相同，这种工艺称为完全退火，它消除了所有工序遗留的结构缺陷，细化了晶格，使金属变软。退火还可以释放金属中残留的内应力。

退火并不是最适合低碳钢的热处理方法。经过完全退火的低碳钢硬度过低，强度相对也小，使得其对切削的阻力小，但是由于其有足够的塑性和韧性，切削时会拉伤和磨损已加工表面，使表面质量变差，因此切削加工性差。然而，多数高碳钢和合金钢通常能通过退火极大地提高其机械加工性。除非是在软化的情况下，否则由于它们的硬度、强度太高会很难切削。购买的工具钢一般是退火态的，有时有必要对硬化后的钢再次加工，则必须对其进行退火处理。为了尽可能使钢变软并获得最好的韧性，冷却速度应该十分缓慢，例如可以随加热炉一起冷却。碳含量越高，则冷却速度必须越慢。

正火的目的通常是细化晶体结构，这些晶体因锻造而变得粗大。对于多数中碳钢，无论是否在其中加入合金，极力推荐在其被锻造后和机械加工前进行正火处理，从而产生更为均匀的组织，而且在多数情况下还可改善切削加工性。大多数商业钢在轧辊和铸造之后需要正火，但高合金气冷钢不需要进行正火处理，因为进行正火处理后将使材料硬化而失去原有的性能。正火是将金属加热到高于临界温度大概55～100℃后使其自然冷却。

淬火是一种最古老最有效的金属硬化工艺，其目的是为了获得马氏体。4 种常用的冷却介质按冷却能力降序排列分别是盐溶液、水、油和空气。高温差所产生的高应力会导致扭曲和开裂，所以仅形成淬火所需的结构。需要注意的是，散热必须均匀，以尽量减少不均匀散热产生的热应力。有两种特殊类型即等温淬火和分级淬火，这两种淬火可以减少淬火应力，减小变形和开裂的倾向，在这两种方法中，是淬火钢在选定的较低温度下进行的盐溶液冷却使得淬火的零件达到预期的物理性能。

迅速淬火后得到的钢很脆，应用十分有限，回火可以降低硬度和脆性，使材料满足工作条件。随着这些特性的降低，钢的抗拉强度同时降低，但延展性和韧性有所提高。尽管这种方法(回火)也可将钢软化，但它与退火有很大差别，因为这种方法(回火)适于精确地控制材料的物理性能，而且在多数情况下回火钢没有退火钢那么软。充分淬火的钢经回火所得到的最终结构称为回火马氏体。该结构的变化程度取决于回火温度，重新加热造成的性能变化。温度越高，影响越大，因此选择多大的回火温度一般取决于愿意牺牲多少零件的硬度、强度来换得韧性及延展性。

向钢质工件表面添加碳和随后进行的硬化操作是热处理的重要过程，称为表面硬化。这个过程包括使用熔融氰化钠混合物，用活性固体材料例如木炭、焦炭，或者用能够提供碳原子的气体、油类和干的氰化物填满渗碳介质。

1.7 模 具 材 料

一副模具可能含有 10 多种钢，以及一些有色金属和特种耐热合金。

那些仅仅起轴承导向作用的模具零件是由非铁金属材料如磷青铜或中碳钢制成的。

推出机构和侧抽芯机构必须在模具温度不停变化的状态下流畅地工作。组件中推板和推流道杆的材料是低碳钢(软钢)，含碳量大约为 0.15%。支承和引导模具，以及承受冲击载荷的导柱和止推设备由低碳钢经表面硬化制成。有时为了获得更大的强度也用镍钢经表面硬化制成，但不承受强烈的热冲击，其材料通常是中碳钢。这些零件也可以用铸钢或球墨铸铁制成。通常衬套由渗碳钢制成。

模板的材料通常是中碳钢，例如英国标准中规定 BS970 08M40(En8)，含碳 0.4%，含锰 0.8%，含硅 0.3%。有时也用预硬化钢，其成分是 0.35%C，1.0%Mn，0.5%Si，1.65%Cr，0.5%Cu，这种成分在美国钢铁学会标准中第 20 页提到。

模具镶块、型芯和型腔必须能够承受熔融金属的冲击和高温，其由进行过渗氮或其他能增强耐磨性和耐热性处理的合金钢制成。

项目 2 成 型 设 备

2.1 压 力 机

冲压加工过程是指压力机在很短的间隔时间里，通过模具在工件材料上施加很大压力，从而使工件材料产生剪切或变形。可以在很短的时间内加工出精度较高的零件，压力加工中的工作压力是由压力机产生、导向和控制的。存储在曲柄压力机的旋转飞轮中的能量或者由水压机的液压系统提供的能量被传递给滑块，从而使滑块做直线运动。

基本上，压力机主要包括如下元件：机身、工作台和往复运动的滑块。滑块利用安装在滑块和工作台、打料装置和气垫上的特殊工具即模具对材料施加力。机身是在中心开有口的矩形框架，用来支撑工作台。钢制工作台面厚度一般为 50～130mm，模具和相关零件安装在上面。工作台具有标准尺寸和开口，其可以从压力机制造商处获得。滑块在压力机的上半部分，它在一个行程中移动的距离由压力机的设计尺寸决定。除了水压机外，多数压力机上的滑块的位置可以调整，但行程不可调节。从工作台顶端到滑块(滑块分别处于行程最低和回复至行程最高的两个位置)底部之间的距离，称为压力机的闭合高度。打料装置是压力机向上行程中的一个装置，从压力机上排出工件或废料。气垫是装在压力机工作台下或内部的附件，可以产生向上的运动或力，由空气、油压、橡皮、弹簧或其他组合机构来驱动。

下面是在工业方面应用较多的几种压力机。

(1) 开式双柱可倾压力机(图 2.1)，C 形机架可相对机座倾斜一定角度，可以通过重力处理成型零件。开式压力机允许条料、工件或成型零件从前到后进给或卸料。

(2) 闭式压力机在机身后面有一立柱，上面具有矩形进料口，允许条料、工件进给或卸料。

(3) 水压式压力机广泛应用于自由锻、挤出成型和钣金件成型加工。另外，它也可用于线材拉拔、粉末冶金、塑料成型和特殊成型方式。水压机的滑块由液压缸和活塞来驱动，液压缸和活塞是高压液压或者液压气动系统的组成部分。经过快速的起始速度，与上模连接的滑块缓慢移动对金属工件施加力进行挤压。挤压速度可以精确地控制在金属流动速度允许的范围内，对生产精密锻件特别有利，而且工作压力和行程可以调整，这也是液压机的优势。

(4) 双动式压力机主要用于金属零件的深拉深成形。这种压力机有两个机械驱动滑块：压边滑块和冲压滑块。压边圈呈矩形空心片状，并由立柱导向。冲压滑块安装在中空的压边圈上并沿其上下移动。这两个滑块由一个集中的驱动器驱动，包括一个驱动离合器和制动。在一个典型的生产行程中，当离合器被驱动时，压边下降快于冲压下降。压边接触工件，压边圈压住时，然后冲压滑块在冲压力下平稳向下，完成冲压工作。压边圈同时压住，以防止它起皱。

(5) 三动式压力机和双动式压力机一样也有内、外滑块，但它在工作台里还有另一个滑块，该滑块可向上运动，从而在一个冲压循环中产生反向拉伸。

(6) 肘式压力机用于印花工艺，驱动的设计允许在滑动行程的底部有非常高的冲压力，这种型号的压力机(肘式压力机)采用曲柄，该曲柄通过移动一个由两根在死点之间来回摆动的连杆构成的接头，从而使得滑块在冲程末端运行速度减慢，产生一个短且有力的运动。

(7) 压弯成形机除了机身比较大外(多为1.8～2m或更大)，基本上类似于开式压力机。压弯成形机主要用在大的条料上实现弯曲操作，也可以通过压力模具实现一系列冲孔、切边、成形等分离操作。压弯成形机可以将复杂的零件准确地加工出来，而不需要高成本的压力模具，这主要通过将复杂的零件操作工艺分成几个单独操作来实现。此种类型的操作常常用在小批量生产或样品试制中，模具成本一般比较低，但是由于零件的定位与传递在每一个位置都是由人工操作的，人力成本相对比较高。

在压力机的设计方面，操作者的安全也是必须注意的一个基本问题。在滑块下方放置的安全滑块必须能阻止滑块的惯性下落，滑块应锁定在一个 Off 位置。在压力机运行期间，合理防护和安全措施必须随时跟进。

2.2 注射成型机

大量的塑料制品是采用注射成型工艺生产的。(注射)过程是：首先经过计量和熔化阶段从给料斗进给粉末状或粒状的塑料混合物，然后再将其注射到模具中。经过短暂的冷却阶段后，打开模具，固化的塑料零件被推出。常用注射成型机的主要部件如图2.2所示。

目前单级往复螺杆式注射装置(图2.3)应用更广泛，因为它塑化物料更彻底，而且塑化效率也较高。螺杆集注射装置与塑化装置的作用于一体，当将物料加入到旋转的螺杆中时，物料依次经过3个区域，分别为加料区、压缩区、定量区。在加料段之后，螺杆的螺槽深度将逐渐变浅，从而对塑料产生压实力，所做的功通过对塑料的剪切作用转化为加热塑料的热能，使塑料成为粘流态。在定量段，来自于料筒表面的热传导获得额外的热能。当螺杆前方的空腔被塑料填满时，会迫使螺杆向后退，断开限位开关，启动液压缸，液压缸驱动螺杆向前运动，将液态塑料注射到闭合的模具中，使用一个止逆阀可以阻止塑料在压力作用下倒流回螺槽。

注射模塑材料最早使用的方法是单级柱塞法，如图 2.4 所示。当柱塞后退时，物料从料斗进入加料室，然后柱塞向前挤压物料经过软化塑料的加热室，最后在压力作用下射入模具。在两级预塑式注射装置中(图 2.5)，物料是在一个预塑料筒中塑化的，通过柱塞或螺杆的运动将一定量的塑料传递到注射室，然后柱塞从注射室将塑料注入模具中。

一台注射成型机在一个注射周期中完成对热塑性塑料的加热软化、成型和冷却硬化等过程。工艺温度通常为 150～380℃，注射压力通常取 35～350MPa。模具采用水冷却，以便移走塑件时不变形。当打开模具时，成型的塑件和浇注系统凝料从注射机侧面退出，并从另一侧被顶出。然后模具重新闭合并锁紧，开始进入下一个工作周期。许多往复螺杆式注射机也可以用来加工热固性塑料。很显然，这种塑料通常采用压缩或传递模塑的成型方法。热固性塑料是在模腔内固化或者发生聚合反应后取出的，其温度范围为 190～210℃。由此可见，热固性塑料的注射周期较短，因为其模具只需要被加热，而热塑性塑料注射模具成型时还需要冷却。

注射成型机还可以用于分层的塑料制品成型。一套液压缸将一定量的表层塑料注入模具中，然后另一个液压缸在塑料内部喷射填充物。最后，从第一个液压缸进行的最后喷射将心部的塑料从浇口处分开，其目的就是生产具有最佳性能的分层复合材料，心部和表层的塑料均可被发泡成型。

项目 3　压力成型工艺与模具

3.1　锻　　造

正如人们所知，锻造是最古老的金属加工工艺。在人类文明初期，就发现加热过的金属更容易被锤打成各种不同的形状。锻造就是通过锻打或冲压将金属加工成所需要的形状，通常经过加热金属的塑性可以得到改善。采用锻造方法加工的锻件的重量为 0.5 千克到 200 多吨，通常使用汽锤、空气锤或摇锤、液压机。在大多数情况下，需要将锻造的金属加热到锻造温度，但有时也可进行冷锻。冷锻是在室温到金属的临界温度范围内完成的。

一般金属可以通过如下 3 种基本锻造工艺锻造：拔长、镦粗和挤压。锻造可按下面 4 种主要方法进行分类：手工锻造、落锤锻造、压力机锻造和镦粗。

对具有同样化学成分的锻件和铸件进行比较，锻件的力学性能一般比铸件要好，原因至少有以下 3 个。

① 合理控制纤维流线方向可以提高金属强度。

② 锻造过程可以得到致密的组织，通常能避免缩孔、气泡和缩松的产生。

③ 锻造有助于细化金属的晶粒，锻造加工使金属沿结晶面产生滑移，从而使粗晶粒细

化。因此，那些需承受剧烈内应力的零件更适合通过锻造成型。

只有当锻件的最后形状确定后，生产给定锻件所需的工具才能制作出来。所以，对模具设计者来说掌握锻模设计的基本原理是非常重要的。模具设计者要考虑到以下几个方面：锻模斜度、分型面、倒角半径、收缩率和模具磨损量，以及模具错配、配合公差和加工余量。

当确定锻件分型面时，必须考虑到金属的流动性以及所产生的纤维流线的方向。如果可能，应该尽量选择水平方向上的平直分型面，因为不规则的分型面可能造成压力(中心)的偏移，而且会增加模具的成本。标准拔模斜度是 7 度，过小的拔模斜度会引起模具的快速磨损，增加锻件粘模的可能性。因为锻造时为了冷却，几股冷却液冲向锻模，锻件将沿着模具内表面收缩，所以内拔模斜度要求大一些，通常是 10 度。

无拔模斜度锻造常用于锻造非铁金属及合金。模具通常安装在成套冲模中，在锻造压力机下工作。根据锻件的外形，模具型腔的两块或更多块是可以移动的，这提高了锻造的通用性，但生产率较低。在许多情况下，坯料第一次锻压时没有完全闭合，多余的材料被切除，然后坯料被再次加热进行第二次锻压，此时模具完全闭合。

锻造用的模具必须能够承受巨大的应变力，抵抗磨损，将裂纹抑制到最小程度，而且在大量生产的条件下有较长的寿命。为了能具备以上性能，模具材料采用铬-镍-钼合金钢、铬-镍合金钢或者铬-钼合金钢。

3.2 冲裁原理

本书将会经常使用一些模具专业术语。图 3.1 所示为一些常见的术语。

利用凹凸模切割金属是一个剪切过程(图 3.2)，在这个过程中，位于两个刃口处的金属承受的剪切应力达到了断裂点，即超过了材料的极限应力。金属承受拉应力和压应力。在超出弹性极限时伸长，然后进入塑性变形，断面减小，最终裂纹沿不断减小的断面上的撕裂带扩展，从而实现完全分离。

处于金属上部的凸模施压使金属变形并进入凹模入口。当继续加载超出材料的弹性极限时，金属的一部分将被压入凹模入口，在材料下表面形成压痕，上表面也相应地发生变形。当载荷继续增加时，凸模将把金属压入到某一个深度，直至压入凹模的深度等于金属的厚度。这个压入过程发生在剪切引起的断裂开始和金属横截面减小之前，在上、下剪切刃处缩小的断面上均出现裂纹。如果(凹凸模)间隙适于所需冲裁的材料，这些断口将相互扩展直至最终相遇，从而引起材料完全分离。凸模继续下行将冲下的部分通过料架推入凹模的漏料孔(图 3.3)。

如果所冲裁的零件是不规则形状，滑块中心两侧的剪切力的总和将不会相等。这种不规则形状将导致压力机滑块处在弯曲力矩的作用下产生偏斜和变形。因此，寻找一个能使剪切力的总和对称(平衡)的点是很有必要的，这个点就称为压力中心，它是冲裁轮廓线参数的中心，而不是(封闭区域内)面积的重心。设计冲裁工具时应保证将其安装在压力机上时压力中心落在压力滑块的轴线上，如图 3.3 所示。

间隙是一副模具凸、凹模之间的配合空间。剪切刃之间的合理间隙可以确保裂纹汇合。剪切刃的撕裂部分将形成一条具有合理间隙的光亮带。为了保证剪切刃的最佳精度，设置合理的间隙是必要的，其大小取决于冲压成型材料的种类、厚度、韧度(硬度)(图 3.4)。毛坯的剪切断面的上部拐角与落料件的下部拐角都将形成一个圆角,在此恰好是凸、凹模口接触材料的区域。这个圆角半径是由于材料发生塑性变形引起的,并且在冲裁比较软的金属材料时圆角半径会更大。过大的间隙将在这些拐角处形成更大的圆角,而在相对的另一面拐角处出现大的毛刺。

压力机的吨位是剪切和成型零件所需要的力加上考虑 30%安全因素的力的总和。在很多情况下,如果使用弹簧驱动的卸料装置,还必须加上卸料力,因为在冲剪材料时压力机必须有压缩弹簧。相应地,对于任何用于成型、拉深凸缘(防皱)及类似用途的弹簧力都应加上弹簧力。

3.3 冲孔模与落料模

1. 冲孔模

任何一副完整的冲压模具都是由生产冲压零件的配合零件组成的,同时还包括模具上的固定支承零件和传力连接零件。在压力加工术语中通常把所有冲压模具上的凹件定义为凹模(图 3.5、图 3.6)。

导柱安装在下模座上。上模座安装与导柱滑动配合的导套。上、下模座连同导柱、导套组合成的部件称为模架。市场上有多种模架尺寸和设计形式供选用。

安装在上模座上的凸模固定装置用来固定凸模。有时,安装在一个细小凸模外围的套筒可以防止凸模在滑块压力作用下弯曲。冲孔模中的凸模应冲出所要求的孔径。

废料或工件粘在上行的凸模上时,必须从凸模上卸掉废料。弹簧驱动的卸料板相对凹模板运动,将原材料卸下,直到凸模从冲过的孔内抽出。被冲孔的工件用定位板定位,定位板是与冲件外形轮廓相符的平板。在滑块下行之前,毛坯要在凹模内通过定位销、定位板或其他类型的定位装置定位。

2. 落料模

除了用一块凹模板代替凹模衬套和用一个落料凸模代替两个冲孔凸模,坯料的定位用定位板代替外,小型落料模具的设计与冲孔模具的设计类似。由于冲出的落料件经凹模、下模座和压力机垫板内孔下落,所以这是一副下出料方式的结构设计。

大型落料件倒装工通常采用落料模,其凹模被安装在上模座,而凸模被固定在下模座。通过垫板的下出料方式来实现大型落料件通常是不切实际的,而采用镶拼式结构设计则比较合适。

对于倒装式落料模,漏料孔斜度或倾斜角处的间隙是不必要的,因为落料件不会采用下出料方式。为了使冲裁刃口结构简单,便于修磨,保证强度,每一个拼块不应该存在刃口轮廓线的交点和复杂轮廓,其他 6 个拼块包含了所有的直线轮廓。

弹簧驱动的卸料装置固定在下模座,它向上运动可以从固定在下模座上的凸模上卸掉废料,卸料螺栓对卸料动作起固定和导向作用。

在压力机滑块回程时,推杆的上端将撞到固定在压力机机身上的打杆,推杆下端向下施力,通过模具使冲制的零件从模腔内被推下。限位环用来挡住推杆并限制它的运动行程。

3. 复合模

在压力机的一次单行程中,复合模只完成冲裁工艺(通常为冲孔和落料)。复合模可以生产平面度和尺寸公差精度较高的冲孔落料件。复合模的特征是落料凸模与落料凹模是倒装的。如图 3.8 所示，落料凹模被固定在上模座，而落料凸模则被固定在下模座。落料凸模同时也起到冲孔作用，在下模座及冲孔凹模内有一个锥形孔作为漏料孔。

在压力机滑块的上行程中，压力机的打料杆撞击打料环，推动打料杆和卸料块下移，从而将成品件从落料凹模中推出。条料由固定在卸料装置上的导料板导向。当卸料板向上运动时，将从落料凸模上卸下废料。在冲裁操作开始前，板料在卸料板与落料凹模的下平面之间被压平。

四个特殊的卸料螺钉在工业上是通用零件。该螺钉在卸料板的卸料行程中起导向和固定预压弹簧的作用。

落料凹模与凸模衬套用螺纹连接，并用销子固定在上模座上。

当弹性推件杆从凹模内推出落料件时，在推件块上装的弹性顶料销(油封击破器)被压下。在滑块上行时，顶料销击破落料件和顶料销的表面油封，使零件从落料凹模内落下。

3.4 弯 曲 模

弯曲是沿平板料或条料位于中性面内的中心线(通常为沿长度方向)发生的均匀变形(图 3.10)。中性层是在弯曲材料上变形为零的平面。金属的流动发生在金属的塑性变形范围内，因而当撤销所施加的外力后，金属的弯曲也会保留一个永久的形状。弯曲件内表面呈现压缩变形，外表面呈现拉伸变形。变通弯曲变形不可能在被弯曲的金属材料上准确地再现凸、凹模的形状。

弯曲半径：最小弯曲半径因材料而异，通常，退火状态的金属材料能被弯曲到与材料相等的半径而不会发生弯裂现象。

弯曲件的展开长度：由于弯曲后被弯金属会变长，如果弯曲件的长度公差非常关键，则模具设计者也必须考虑其增长的长度。弯曲金属的长度可用如下公式计算：

$$B = \frac{A}{360} 2\pi (R_i + Kt)$$

B：弯曲沿中性轴展开长度(mm)；

A：弯曲中心角()；

R_i：弯曲件内表面半径(mm)；

t：材料厚度(mm)；

K：0.33($R_i<2t$)或 0.5($R_i>2t$)。

V 形弯曲：用 V 形块支撑的金属条料或板料(图 3.11)，在楔形凸模的作用下进入 V 形块内。这种方法使弯曲件成形为锐角、钝角或直角。在 V 形凹模内，弹簧加载钩销和零件间的摩擦会防止或减小零件在弯曲时的侧移。

打弯：打弯是对横梁的悬臂部分加载(图 3.11)，弯曲凸模 1 施压在金属上，使之背靠凹模块 2。弯曲件的中心线平行于凹模边缘。在凸模接触坯料之前，坯料被弹性压料板 3 压紧在凹模块上，以防止在凸模下行时金属窜动。

弯曲力：U 形弯曲力大致是 V 形弯曲力的两倍；打弯力为 V 形弯曲的 1/2。

回弹：当作用在金属上的弯曲力去除后，弹性应力也随之消失，这样就引起了金属移动(弹性回弹)，导致弯曲角减小，即弯曲零件的包角增大。这种金属材料的移动称为回弹。

钢材的回弹角在 0.5°～5°范围内变化，这主要取决于金属材料的硬度。磷青铜的回弹角可达到 10°～15°。

V 形弯曲模具的回弹补偿原则为 V 形块或楔形凸模的弯曲小于零件需要的弯曲中心角。由于零件弯曲时比需要的弯曲中心角稍大，因此回弹后可得到需要的弯曲角。

项目 4　塑料成型工艺与模具

4.1　注　射　模　具

注射模具的原理与铸造模具的相似(图 4.1)。塑料粉末被加入注射机料斗后，柱塞或螺栓拉回，一定量的塑料粉末被送入注射机料筒内后经高温和压力的作用变成熔体。合模后柱塞或螺栓向前移动，塑化好的塑料熔体在压力作用下进入模具型腔。模具通过循环水冷却后使得塑件冷却固化。开模后制件在推出机构作用下取出塑件。模具内表面是镀铬层。尽管在热固性材料注射成型方面取得了一些进步，但注射模具主要还是用来生产热塑性制件。热固性塑料注射成型的主要问题在于熔融态的热固性塑料可在较短时间内发生固化和硬化。

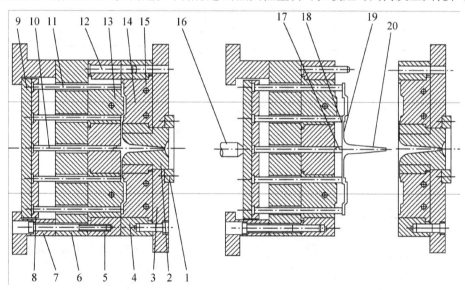

图 4.1　传统两板式模具

1—定位圈；2—浇口套；3—底板；4—型腔定板；5—型芯定板；6—支撑板；7—模脚；8—推杆固定板；9—推板；10—拉料杆；11—推杆；12—导柱；13—型芯(凸模)镶件；14—型腔(凹模)镶件；15—水道；16—活塞杆；17—冷料井；18—内浇口；19—流道；20—浇口

注射模具具有如下优点。
(1) 可适应大批量生产的较快成型速度。
(2) 具有多种可提供有效使用性能的热塑性材料。
(3) 可成型螺纹、侧凹、侧孔和大的薄截面。

4.2 压缩模

在压缩成型中塑料粉末或预制件被放入热的金属模具型腔中(图 4.2)。由于分型面是水平面，上模可竖直下降，合模后加热加压一段时间，使塑料呈熔融态并充满整个型腔。尽管最近开发的醇酸树脂可在 25 秒内完成固化，一般的塑料固化时间都要在 1～15 分钟内。开模后取出制件。如果制件中设计有金属嵌体，需在加料前用销钉或孔将嵌体定位在型腔内。同样的预制件在放入型腔前需预热以减少气体、提高熔融态塑料的流动性和减少固化时间。目前预热预制件最方便的方法是电加热。

在加热和加压的作用下会硬化的热固性塑料也可以采用压缩成型和传递成型的方法(图 4.3)。而热塑性材料不适用于压缩成型工艺，这是因为针对热塑性塑料的压缩模具需要交替地加热和冷却，使得生产周期变长。为了节约材料，不需要设计浇口和流道，因为切掉浇口和流道的成型材料将损失热固性塑料。压缩成型所需的压力机通常是立式液压压力机。

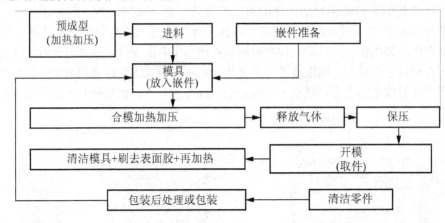

图 4.2 压缩成型过程

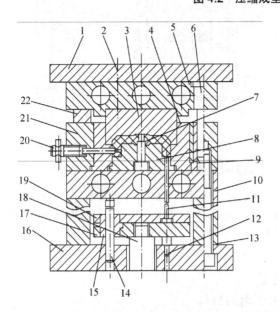

1—上模板；2—螺栓；3—凹模；
4—凸模镶块；
5、10—凹凸模固定板(含加热圈)；
6—导柱；7—凸模镶件/入子；
8—凸模；9—导套；11—推杆；
12—限位钉；13—垫板；
14—推杆导柱；15—推杆导柱导套；
16—下模座；17—推板；18—尾杆；
19—推杆固定板；20—侧型芯；
21—凹模固定板；22—承压板

图 4.3 典型的压缩成型模具

4.3 注射系统主要部件

推料杆和圆弹簧常被用于一般注射模具中(图 4.4)，推料杆和气弹簧有时也用于大型注射模具中(图 4.5)。

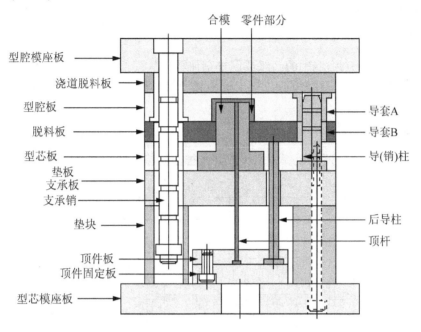

图 4.4 一般注射模具示例

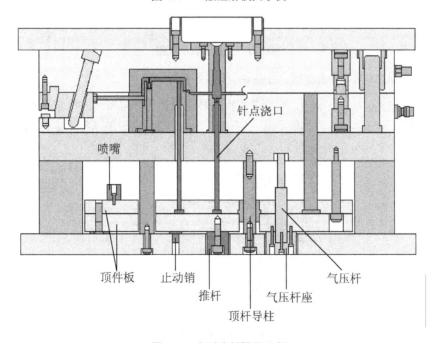

图 4.5 大型注射模具示例

1. 顶出板制动装置(行程终端销，如图4.6所示)

它是阻止顶出板向前运动的障碍物(止动销)。

2. 浇口锁销

浇口锁销有一个侧向分型的边，这样在模具打开时可拉出零部件，并从浇口套中除去一个浇口。模具打开后，缩销将起到顶出销的作用并从浇口套中推出浇口，同时释放出已融化塑料中的气体。

3. 顶出板

顶出板支撑推顶杆(顶出销)的边缘或回推销使零件从模具中被推出。在模具夹紧过程中，当回推销的边缘撞到型腔板时，推出板由成型机的脱模器装置推出并返回到最初的位置。

4. 止动销

已安装的制动装置使顶出板保持水平或防止推出器模板(顶出板)退离过远以及破坏型芯安装板。

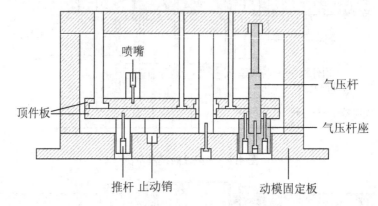

图4.6 注射系统示意图

5. 顶出导销(脱模器导销)/顶出导套(脱模器导套)(如图4.7所示)

顶出导销也被称为推板导销，起到顶出板的导轨槽作用。因为顶出导套滑动，所以使用较硬的材料。顶出导套也被称为推板导套，它是一个通过与顶出导销匹配来定位的圆柱形部件。

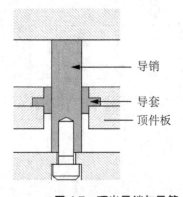

图4.7 顶出导销与导管

6. 推杆(如图 4.8 所示)

连接在注塑机上的轴可产生(液压或机械)力使顶出板工作。

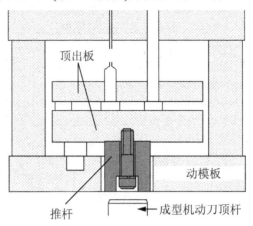

图 4.8　推杆

7. 气压弹簧/气压弹簧支架(如图 4.9 所示)

气压弹簧可用力退回顶出板。弹簧的强度可通过充气压力调节。当使用气压弹簧时，一定要避免高温(因为热量可能会使气体膨胀并破坏气压弹簧的最初功能)。气压弹簧支架是用于把气压弹簧固定到顶出板的部件。因为它能起到推杆的作用，所以具有用于螺栓连接的沉孔工艺。

项目 5　计算机在工业中的应用

5.1　CAD/CAM

自从计算机技术出现至今，制造业技术人员一直希望自动化产品的设计过程，并通过建立起来的相关数据库实现制造过程的自动化。CAD/CAM 的关键目标(图 5.1)是使建立起来的产品设计数据库可同时应用于产品的制造。当数据库被成功创建时，传统上存在于零部件设计和制造之间的障碍就可以消除了。CAD/CAM 技术可以共享零部件设计和制造之间的通用数据资料。

CAD/CAM 技术出现后，相应地也出现了其他一些术语。

(1) 计算机辅助设计与制造(CAD/CAM)。

(2) 计算机辅助工程(CAE)。

(3) 计算机图形学(CG)。

(4) 计算机辅助工艺规划(CAPP)。

(5) 计算机辅助设计和绘图(CADD)。

这些新兴的术语涉及到 CAD/CAM 概念的各个特定方面。CAD/CAM 本身就是一个广泛的、涵盖面很广的术语。它处在自动化和集成化制造的核心位置。

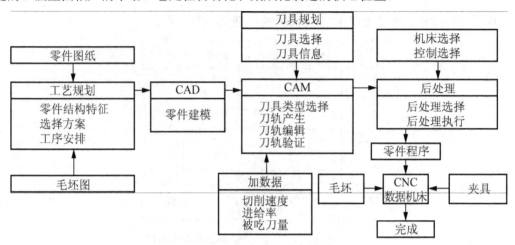

图 5.1 CAD/CAM 系统结构图

交互式计算机图形学(ICG)在计算机辅助设计与制造中起着重要作用。通过使用计算机图形交互技术，在存储电子形式的图像数据时设计师在可以绘制所要设计的产品图像。图形图像可以以二维、三维或实体格式的形式表现。交互式计算机图形图像由基本的点、直线、圆弧和曲线构成。图形图像一旦创建，可以通过多种方式对其进行简单的编辑和复制，包括放大、缩小、旋转和移动。交互式计算机图形系统由以下 3 部分组成。

(1) 硬件：包括计算机和很多外围设备。

(2) 软件：包括计算机程序和相关技术手册(流行的交互式计算机图形软件包括 AutoCAD、UG、Pro/E、I-DEAS 和 CATIA 等)。

(3) 设计者：三个组成部分中最重要的一个。

CAD/CAM 的应用可不断提高企业的生产效率和竞争力。CAD/CAM 技术的优点在于：可提高生产率；获得的产品质量更好；通信更便捷；提供通用的产品制造数据资料；制作样品的费用减少；可以更快地响应客户要求。

5.2 CAD/CAM 的应用

1. CAD 技术的优势

在绘图和设计工作中应用计算机技术的好处是十分显著的：可提高速度，精度高，减少硬拷贝存储空间，调用速度较快，可增强通信功能，提高绘图质量且图形容易修改。

2. 计算机辅助数控编程

数控编程软件使得数控编程变得更加容易，尤其是需要计算大量刀位的复杂零件的编程。编程软件是 CAM 软件包中的一个软件，它有一个动态的图形数据库，可以支持实际的加工工序。这些加工工序可以被显示、编辑、串联或删除。不管是单个切削还是 CNC 循环指令程序均可以通过编程软件完成程序设计。软件还自动为加工计算合适的进给量和切削速度，生成刀轨列表，定义刀具路径。

3. 数控刀具路径验证

在零件被加工前,为了减少实际加工中可能出现的错误,需要对零件程序进行验证。零件程序验证有很多种方法:在机床上空运行程序检验总体程序中的错误;通过加工蜡、塑料、木头、泡沫或其他材料的样品来检验产品的几何外形。当零件加工程序是使用CAD/CAM 系统生成的时候,可以使用实体模型生成一幅工件、刀具、切削路径以及成品的逼真图片。切削过程的实时模拟画面可以显示在屏幕上。大多数模拟都是基于几何形状的模拟,并没有考虑切削的具体情况。

4. 计算机辅助工艺规划

工艺规划是设计与制造之间的关键桥梁,设计信息只有通过工艺规划才能被转换成制造语言。计算机辅助工艺规划有如下优点:减少对有经验设计者的需求,减少时间和成本;生成更一致和准确的规划;提高生产效率。

5. 成组技术

在 CAD 系统中图形被存储在数据库中。成组技术提供的组件都带有图形号码。每个图形的代码都是由一个代码系统来分配的,每个数字都有含义。如果编码序号已知,在没有图纸的情况下可以推断出组件的许多功能。

6. 库存管理

库存管理已实行一段时间,但是借助于计算机可以获得更准确的信息,制造系统能够更加容易地对改变做出响应。可以直接从 CAD 系统中获得物料清单,清单信息包括库存号、目录名、库存量、计算单位、最小库存量、外购或自制的提前时间和每个零件和供应商的具体说明。

7. 机器人

工业机器人是由计算机程序控制的机械手。改变程序就会改变行动的执行顺序。机械手(工业机器人)被广泛用于盘式和直线式传输中的自动装配操作中。

8. 计算机集成制造

计算机集成制造是用来表述现代加工方法的术语。CIM(计算机集成制造)包含许多先进的制造技术,例如 CNC(计算机数控)、CAD/CAM、工业机器人技术和即时交货技术。集成意味着系统可以提供完整的和即时的信息共享功能。在计算机集成制造系统中,不仅制件可以在计算机中加工和并在机床间自动移动,而且加工操作的顺序可以自动生成。

9. 柔性制造系统

装配线和传输线(图 5.2)均属于刚性自动化领域。与刚性自动化相反,程序自动化是柔性的,能够处理各种类型的制件。图清晰地显示了两个自动化成功应用的领域。大批量的传输线(刚性自动化)与小批量的单个 NC 或 CNC 的柔性生产间存在差距。差距包括一定产品设计导致的中等批量。客户定制的产品要求柔性和中等批量。可行的方法是结合刚性自动化和程序自动化的优点,准确地讲是柔性制造系统。

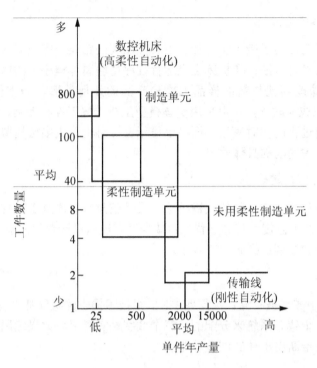

图 5.2 装配线和传输线

练习
1. 计算机数控　2. 计算机辅助设计　3. 计算机辅助制造　4. 计算机集成制造
5. 柔性制造系统　6. 计算机辅助工艺编制　7. 刚性自动化　8. 刀具路径模拟
9. 提前时间

项目 6　模具的制造技术

6.1　NC/CNC 的应用

数字控制(NC)是按照含有机床刀具运动信息的程序所指定的顺序自动执行操作的加工过程。数字控制的概念是 20 世纪 40 年代末由密歇根州特拉弗斯城的约翰帕森斯提出的。

由计算机控制的数字控制技术称为计算机数字控制(CNC)。对于 NC 和 CNC 来说，其工作原理是相同的，只有命令执行的控制方式不同。计算机是 CNC 机床的控制单元，它们内嵌于计算机中或通过通信通道与数控机床连接。当程序员将一些信息以程序的形式输入磁带等中后，计算机将使用所有需要的数据进行计算以完成工作。

自从面世以来，NC 技术就在很多方面有了应用，包括车床、车削中心、铣床和加工中心、冲压机、电火花加工(EDM)、线切割、磨床、试验检测仪器等。最复杂的计算机数控机床是车削中心，如图 6.1 所示(一个具有十转位的刀架能进行快速换刀的现代车削中心，按下按钮后,可在数秒内定位每个刀具)。还有加工中心,如图 6.2(立式加工中心,刀具库在机器左边,右边的控制面板可由操作人员旋转)和图 6.3(卧式加工中心,有自动换刀装置,刀具库可安放 200 套切削工具)所示。

当为某一特定操作编写程序时,程序员必须利用推荐值选择所有的切削参数,包括切削进给速度、进给率、刀具种类及几何尺寸等。当程序员选择完所有必要参数后,操作员将程序输入机器,然后按开始按钮以进行切削加工。数控机床可自动地完成从一次切换命令加工到另一个命令、转换切削刀具以及提供冷却液。在非常短的时间内,工件在高质量的标准下被加工成型。此外不管工作量有多大,所有制件都可以等值等量地完成。这样的先进技术,由于其在表面质量和组件公差方面具有优势而被许多行业所追捧,如航空航天、核子核能以及医疗设置的制造,只有 CNC 机床才能加工出最满足要求的产品。

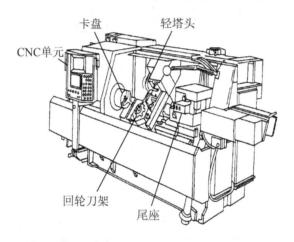

图 6.1　具有十转位刀架可快速换刀的现代车削中心

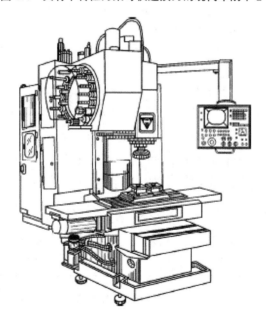

图 6.2　立式加工中心

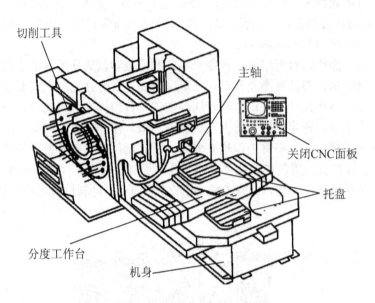

图 6.3 卧式加工中心

6.2　NC 操作控制面板

1. 紧急停止(E-STOP，图 6.4)

当按下这个按钮后，进给或旋转的刀具将停止且计算机控制系统将关闭。E-STOP 按钮只能在一些特殊情况下使用，例如机床过载、某一机器零件松动或程序中不正确的数据导致刀具和工件冲突等。为了重设 E-STOP 按钮，按下它并顺时针转动，机器将再次启动，归零后排出掉迫使按 E-STOP 按钮的原因。

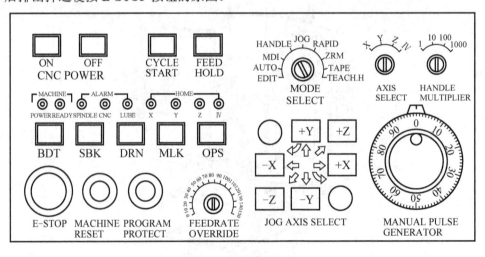

图 6.4　操作控制面板

2. 模式选择

此开关的布置详细显示了其操作模式(不论是计算机控制还是手动控制)。

(1) 在 EDIT(工程设计智能终端)模式下可以进行如下工作。

① 将程序输入机床存储器中。
② 修正程序。
③ 将数据从程序转化为数据磁带。
④ 检查存储器的存储能力。

(2) AUTO(自动)模式可使得存储的 NC 命令得以执行。

(3) MDI(人工数据输入)模式可以利用以程序段形式输入的信息来自动控制加工过程，而不与基本程序发生干扰。这个模式经常用于工件夹紧装置的加工。人工数据输入适于像铣平面和钻孔这样的单一加工运动，这类单一加工运动的描述信息不需要输入到内存中。

MDI 模式还可以在运行程序过程中使用。例如，假设在程序中忘记了命令 S350 M03，为了纠正这一错误，打开单程序段开关(SBK，见图 6.4)，然后将位置指向 MDI 模式。

(4) HANDLE(手动)模式允许利用手动转轮(手动脉冲发射器，见图 6.4)沿着 X、Y、Z、B 中的任一个轴方向来手动控制工作台的运动。利用顺时针转动手轮，可以使刀具沿相对于坐标系统的正方向移动。在手动操作机床时，使用附加速度开关(手动变速钮，如图 6.4 所示)可改变手动转轮每个刻度的位移量。

(5) JOG(点动进给)模式允许选择沿着 X、Y、Z 轴方向的手动恒定进给量。利用 JOG 模式下的选择开关，就可以使用 JOG AXIS SELECT(点动进给轴选择)按钮和 FEEDRATE OVERRIDE(进给倍率)按钮了。

(6) 按下 ZRM(零点返回)模式后再按按钮 X、Y 或者 Z 可以使刀具回到其轴线的零点位置。

3. 循环开始

在执行内存或者数据纸带中的程序过程中，使用这个按钮。当此按钮被按下后上面的控制灯会打开。

4. 进给锁定

当按下这个按钮后，位于按钮上方的控制灯亮起，而位于 CYCLE START (循环开始)按钮上方的控制灯则关掉，同时所有的进给被中断，但是旋转的命令并没有受到影响。这个按钮应用得很少。在加工螺纹时，当丝锥抽出后 FEED HOLD(进给锁定)生效。如果在加攻螺纹过程中丝锥发生断裂，唯一阻止车床运转的方法就是按下 E-STOP 按钮。

5. 单程序段(SBK)

要运行一个程序段时可打开 SBK 按钮，每当 CYCLE START(循环开始)按钮被按下时，只有一个程序段将被运行。此开关还可以被用于以下两种情况：用户想在机床上对一段新程序执行情况进行检查，或在机床加工过程中瞬时中断。

6. 空运行

打开此按钮后，所有快速的工作进给量都被修改为一个进给量。为了达到这个目的，可以使用 FEEDRATE OVERRIDE(进给倍率)和 DRY RUN(空运行)按钮去检查车床上的一个新的程序，而不用刀具实际去运行。

7. 进给倍率

控制工作进给量必须符合功能指定 F，以增大或减少输入程序的数据百分比。

8. 机床锁定(MLK)

此开关用于检查车床上的一个新程序。当检查在计算机屏幕上显示运行的程序的时候，所有刀具的运作将被锁定。

9. 电源开关

当位于控制系统显眼处的主要能源开关被打开后，控制装置才能打开。而在能源开关关闭之前，就需要将控制装置关闭。

10. 机床复位

MACHINE RESET(机床复位)按钮用于取消警报或者操作。当机床处于工作模式时不能使用复位按钮。

11. 控制面板

CONTROL PANEL(控制面板)一般位于主要电子系统的前部，由一个显示屏和许多开关以及按钮组成(如图 6.5 所示)。

12. 显示器

所有的特征、地址和数据都显示在屏幕上(如图 6.6 所示)。当前运行的程序内容按序号排列(如图 6.7 所示)，而且下一个进度和程序表也会以程序方式显示出来。

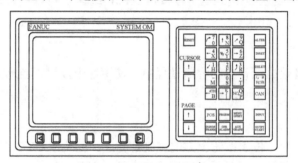

图 6.5　控制面板(FANUC 系统)

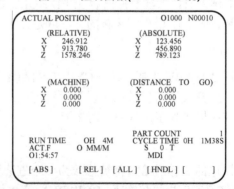

图 6.6　地址显示

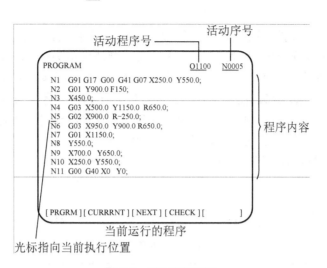

图 6.7 现行程序显示

6.3 NC/CNC 显示屏幕的阅读

屏幕阅读是一项重要技能,并且只有通过实践才能提高。当验证程序和加工第一个零件时,特别需要这项技能。通过屏幕阅读可避免许多严重的问题。

CNC 机床监视器可显示不同的屏幕界面:编程屏幕、位置屏幕、刀具偏置屏幕、工作零点屏幕和参数屏幕。

每一种屏幕显示都提供了许多关于机床状况的有用信息。对于操作者来说最重要的屏幕是刀具偏置和位置屏幕。如果机床具有加工模式转换功能,则加工模式转换屏幕对于机床设置也是重要的。

1. 刀具偏置屏幕

所有车床刀具的偏置都是相似的,同样的道理加工中心刀具偏置屏幕也是相似的。表 6-1 显示的是目前应用广泛的加工中心刀具偏置屏幕的第一页内容。

表 6-1 刀具轴向偏置

编号	长度		半径	
	几何尺寸	磨损	几何尺寸	磨损
001	-19.1900	0.0000	0.0000	0.0000
002	-20.1300	-0.0100	0.0000	0.0000
003	-17.9000	0.0000	0.0000	0.0000
004	-20.7300	0.0000	0.0000	0.0000
005	19.8820	0.0000	0.0000	0.0000
…	…	…	…	…
015	-12.5770	0.0000	0.5000	0.0050
016	…10.2250	0.0000	0.3750	0.0000

表 6-1 最上面显示的是屏幕的名字。屏幕被分成了两部分:长度和半径。它们是刀具轴向偏置量和刀具径向偏置量的缩写。刀具偏置量从 1 排列到 16,几何尺寸一列显示了安

装时输入的偏置量,磨损一列显示了加工过程中刀具偏置量的调整值。

002 号的几何偏置数值为-20.1300,增加的偏置调整值为-0.01,因此其偏置总值为 20.1310。要注意在增量方式下也可以调整几何偏置量,这样其磨损偏置量即为零,这就意味着如果需要偏置调整,就需要选择几何外形或者是磨损量,两者不可兼得(一般选择磨损量)。

015 号径向偏置量为 0.500,磨损量为 0.0050,即此程序要用半径为 0.5 英尺的刀具以达到几何偏置值,在加工过程中偏置值可调整 0.005 英尺。或者直接调整几何偏置值为 0.5050,再将磨损量设置为零。同样地,使用磨损量更好些。

2. 位置屏幕

位置屏幕与其他的控件相似。表 6-2 是使用广泛的车床的位置屏幕截图。

表 6-2　位置屏幕

相对位置	绝对位置
U 0.0000 W 0.0000	X 15.5720 Z 5.0210
加工位置	移动距离
X 0.000 Z -749.300	X 0.0000 Z 0.0000

相对位置列显示了刀具相对原位置的距离具体值,可由相对坐标系中的 U 和 W 得到。当读取相对位置数值时,无法确定刀具距离原点的位置,而只能确定刀具距离原位置的距离。坐标系的符号零或者负是因为刀具无法移动得离加工原点过远,所以表 6-2 中数值为零意味着刀具正处于原位置。当为了找到刀具距离原点的实际距离而提刀时,就要用到相对位置的数值了。

绝对位置列的数值为刀具距离原点的绝对距离,该数值可根据绝对坐标系中的 X 和 Y 得到。坐标值符号是正或负,取决于刀具在哪个象限运动。对于加工操作员来说,这个数值非常重要,因为任意一个绝对位置的数值都和制件有关。

6.4　NC 程序

1. NC 机床坐标系

在 NC 系统中,每根轴的运动都备有独立的动力源并以此取代了传统机床上的手轮。驱动源可以是直流电机、步进电机或者液压传动装置。选用何种动力源主要根据机床的精度要求来确定。

机床刀具工作台的运动控制着刀具与工件之间的相对运动。运动的 3 个主轴是 X、Y、Z 轴。使 Z 轴同时垂直于 X 轴和 Y 轴以创建一个右手坐标系。Z 轴的正向定义为刀具离开工件的方向。具体细节如下(如图 6.8 所示)。

(1) Z 轴

① 在一个旋转工件的机床上,如车床,Z 轴平行于主轴,沿正方向的运动驱使刀具远离工件。

② 在一个旋转刀具的机床上，如铣床和镗床，Z轴垂直于刀具安装面，沿正方向的运动驱使刀具远离工件。

③ 其他机床，如冲压、刨床或剪床，Z轴垂直于刀具安装面，沿正方向的运动增大刀具和工件之间的距离。

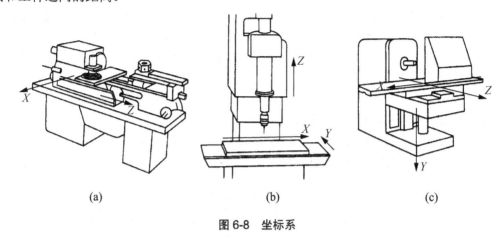

图6-8 坐标系

(a) 车床；(b) 钻床；(c) 铣床

(2) X轴

① 车床上，X轴就是刀具运动的方向，沿正方向的运动使得刀具远离工件。

② 在卧式铣床上，X轴平行于工作面。

③ 在立式铣床上，当程序员面对机床时，X轴正方向指向右侧。

(3) Y轴

Y轴就是标准笛卡儿坐标系中除X、Z轴之外的那个轴。

2. NC机床控制器的基本职能

开启机床之前必须先定义刀具运动的坐标系以及指定是定位运动(快速横向运动)还是进给运动(切削)。进给运动包括直线运动和圆周运动，其中直线运动需要目标位置坐标，如果使用圆弧插补，则需要给定圆心和目标位置坐标。

在进行切断运动之前，要将主轴调整到指定转数/分，同时确定进给速度。主轴既可顺时针方向旋转也可逆时针方向旋转。

有时在加工过程中需要使用冷却液，冷却液有液态的也有薄雾状的。

在带有自动换刀装置的机床上，一把刀具被安装到机床主轴上之前，必须将其编号输入给制器，同时需要确定换刀顺序。

现在倾向于将一些类似钻孔这样具有固定工序的操作集合在一个循环内。使用循环编码可以在很大程度上降低编程量。对于一些特殊循环操作还需要提供些特定信息。

除此之外还有其他程序功能，如英制公制、定位系统——绝对的或者增量的，等等。所有这些都可以有时更要必须通过NC控制器和相关的制件程序进行控制。

这些控制功能总结如下。

(1) Preparatory Functions (预备功能)需指定单位、哪种插补器、绝对还是增量编程、圆弧插补面、刀具补偿等。

(2) Coordinates(坐标系)确定3个空间轴(或转动轴)。

(3) Machining Parameters(加工参数)确定进给以及速度。

(4) Tool Control(刀具控制)确定刀具直径、下一个刀具号、换刀等。

(5) Cycle Functions(循环功能)可指定循环钻孔、循环铰、循环镗、循环铣以及清除表面。

(6) Coolant Control(冷却液控制)可指定冷却液的状态，即冷却液开/关以及是液态还是薄雾态的。

(7) Miscellaneous control(其他控制)可指定其他的一些控制指令，包括打开或关闭主轴、重绕磁带程序、主轴旋转方向、转换托盘以及控制夹具等。

(8) Interpolators(插补器)可确定是直线插补、圆弧插补还是圆心插补。

这些控制功能可由下列程序代码实现。

(1) G-代码(表6-3)又称为预备代码或预备字母。它用来预备实现控制功能的 MCU(机床控制装置/磁性卡片装置/微程序控制器)。

表6-3 常用G-代码

G00	rapid traverse 快速定位，快速横向运动	G40	cutter compensation-cancel 刀补取消
G01	linear interpolation 直线插补	G41	cutter compensation-left 刀具补偿-左刀补
G02	circular interpolation, CW 圆弧插补，顺时针	G42	cutter compensation-right 刀具补偿-右刀补
G03	circular interpolation, CCW 圆弧插补，逆时针	G43	cutter offset positive 刀具正偏值
G04	dwell 暂停	G44	cutter offset cancel 刀具负偏值
G08	acceleration 加速	G80	fixed-cycle cycles 固定循环取消
G09	deceleration 减速	G81~89	fixed cycles 固定循环
G17	X-Y plane XY平面	G90	absolute dimension program 绝对坐标编程
G18	Z-X Plane ZX平面	G91	incremental dimension 增量坐标编程
G19	Y-Z Plane YZ平面	G92	set the workpiece origin 设定工件原点
G20	inch format 英制格式	G96	constant surface speed control 恒线速控制
G21	metric format 米制格式	G97	constant spindle speed control 恒转速控制
G28	return to reference point 返回参考点	G98	feed per minute 每分钟进给
G33	thread cutting 螺纹切削	G99	feed per revolution 每转进给

(2) F-代码用于确定刀具运动的进给速度。这个速度是切削刀具与工件之间的相对速度。其单位为英尺/分钟。如果需要，一个程序里的进给速度也可经常变化。

(3) S-代码用于确定切削速度。切削速度指的就是切削工件的相对表面速度，它是刀具或者工件旋转的结果，因此以单位转数/分进行编写。一些(机床加工数据)手册中给出的这些数据单位为"每分钟表面英尺数"(sfpm)，编程前必须进行转换。如果控制器的编程选项是sfpm，操作工就必须详细说明道具直径。S-代码不开启主轴，主轴由M-代码开户。

(4) T-代码用来编写刀具数目。只有配备自动换刀装置时才会用到此代码。它可指定下一刀具所在刀具库中的位置数目。只有换刀的M-代码被指定后才会实际换刀。

(5) R-代码用来编写循环参数。在确定一个循环钻孔后，需要给定一个净空高度(R面)。R-代码就是用来确定这个净空高度的。

(6) M-代码(见表6-4)称为辅助字符，用来控制机床的多方面功能，包括开启或关闭主轴、开启或关闭机床、开或关冷却液、换刀和重绕磁带程序等。

表 6-4 M-代码

M00	program stop 程序停止	M08	mist clllant on 雾冷状态冷却液开
M01	optional stop 选项停止	M09	coolant off 冷却液开
M02	edn of program 程序结束	M10	chuck close 卡盘夹紧
M03	spindle cw 主轴顺时针转	M11	chuck open 卡盘松开
M04	spindle ccw 主轴逆时针转	M30	end of tape 磁带程序结束
M05	spindle stop 主轴停止	M88	calling of subprogram 调用子程序
M06	tool change 换刀	M99	end of subprogram(return to main program)
M07	fluid coolant on 液冷状态冷却液开		子程序结束，返至主程序

6.5 CNC 机床操作安全守则

在金属切削操作中安全是最需要重视的环节。CNC 设备是自动化的且速度非常快，因此也非常危险。为了防止人身伤害和对设备造成损坏，必须找出危险所在，而且操作人员必须提高警惕注意这些危险。

潜在的危险主要包括：回转件，如主轴、主轴上的刀具、卡盘、卡盘上的工件、转塔车床及一些旋转夹具等；移动件，包括机床中心工作台、车床工作台、尾架中心和刀具旋转式传送带；程序中的错误，包括 G00 代码结合错误坐标值的不正确用法，这将导致难以预见的快速运作；设置或变换偏置量时的错误，这将导致机床上刀具与工件的碰撞；对已验证的程序做不正确的修改也会导致机床的危险运作。

为了减少或避免这些危险，可采取以下预防行动。

(1) 保留所有销售商提供的机床原覆盖物。
(2) 佩戴安全眼镜、手套，穿戴合适的衣物和鞋。
(3) 熟悉机床控制之前不要试图运行。
(4) 运行程序前应确保零件被正确装夹。
(5) 验证程序时，需按照以下安全过程进行。
① 使用 Machine Lock(机床锁定)功能运行程序，验证程序的语法和数值。
② 使用 RAPID OVERRIDE(快速倍率)开关减慢快速的运动或空运行程序。
③ 在运行整个程序前，执行单程序段以确认程序中的每一行命令。
④ 当刀具在切削时，可使用 FEED OVERRIDE(进给倍率)开关减小进给率以防止过量裁切。
(6) 禁止手触切屑和用切屑钩折断长卷曲切削。可编写不同的切削条件程序来更好地控制切削。要清理切屑应先关闭机床。
(7) 如果怀疑刀片在已编入程序的切削条件下可能会断裂，要选择一个更厚的刀片，或减少进给，或减小切削深度。
(8) 悬挂的刀具越短越好，因为它可能成为振动源而弄断刀片。
(9) 若中心支撑了大型制件，应确保孔心足够大以保证能支撑和夹住制件。
(10) 换刀具、标准刀片或移开切屑时要关闭机床。
(11) 置换掉所有变钝或损坏的刀具或刀片。

(12) 记录现行刀具的偏置量并清零。
(13) 未经管理人员同意，不得轻易改动程序。
(14) 若考虑到其他安全事项，应立即通知领导或管理者。

6.6 故障诊断及维修

当出现故障时，需检查事故原因并正确维修。事故排查及维修步骤如下。
(1) 故障何时出现？
(2) 若是自动化操作，程序号、排序号码及程序内容是什么？
(3) 机床是在手动操作模式下还是在特定模式下？
(4) 上一个程序和下一个程序分别是什么？
(5) 是否发生在开关操作中？
(6) 机床系统状况如何？
(7) 是否发生在换刀期间？
(8) 切换到危险诊断界面，检查警报内容。
(9) 驱动放大器状态有无特殊显示？若警报内容与驱动放大器有关，应进行排查！
(10) 机床发出警报的次序能否提供信息？
(11) CRT 屏幕是否正常？
(12) 控制轴是否发生摇摆？
(13) 同类型工作的频率如何？
(14) 故障是否发生在进行相同操作的时候？(重复性检查。)
(15) 改变条件后是否仍会发生故障？(条件包括倍率开关、程序内容、操作顺序等。)

1. 故障范例

(1) 电源无法打开。
检查：插座是否给电？
(2) NC 单元激活后无法操作。
检查：
① 是否选择了正常模式？
② 开启前是否所有条件均符合要求？只有所有预定条件全符合要求后才可以开始操作。查阅机床制造商出版的工作手册进行排查。
③ 倍率开关或手动速度是否设置为零？
④ 不复位，产生了控制进给信号。
⑤ 机床锁定。

2. 报警信息

当按下菜单键 ALARM(报警)后，报警/诊断屏幕将显示如下信息。
(1) 报警
与操作报警、程序错误、伺服警报或者系统错误有关的代码或号码。

(2) 停止代码

在自动运行模式下无法自动运行或或运行停止的状态可以以代码和错误号码的形式显示。

(3) 报警信息

报警信息用内置的用户 PLC 来说明。

(4) 操作信息

操作信息用内置的用户 PLC 来说明。

当发生故障后，代码种类会显示在屏幕上，具体警报类型等信息可参照相关手册。

6.7 控制设备的类型

为了满足如下控制需要，在工业中使用了很多不同种类的控制设备。
(1) Mechanical Control(机械控制器)
(2) Pneumatic Control(气动控制器)
(3) Electromechanical Control(机电控制器)
(4) Electronic Control(电子控制器)
(5) Computer Control(计算机控制器)
(6) Programmable Logic Control (可编程逻辑控制器，PLC)

机械控制器包括凸轮和变阻器，尽管曾被用来控制非常复杂的机器，现如今的机械控制器只用于简单且周期性的任务控制中。一些自动化的机器，如螺纹车床，仍然使用凸轮类型的控制器。由于容易磨损，机械控制器很难生产。

气动控制器在电子管和开关方面应用得非常广泛，可用来构造简单的控制逻辑线路，但速度相对较慢。由于使用了很多标准元件，气动控制器较机械控制器更容易构造逻辑线路。气动控制器零件很容易磨损。

与机械控制器一致，机电控制器使用开关、继电器、定时器、计数器等去构造逻辑线路。由于电流的使用，使得机电控制器更加灵活和快速。使用机电控制器的机器一般称为继电器设备。

电子控制器与机电控制器基本相同，唯一的区别是在机电控制器中活动的机械元件被运行更快、更可靠的电子开关所替代。

计算机控制器是目前最通用的控制系统。其逻辑线路是通过软件编程写入计算机内存中去的。计算机控制器不仅可以控制机床和制造过程的运作，还可以用于数据通信。利用计算机可以编写出具有强大计算能力的非常复杂的控制程序，首先要解决与外界的连接问题。在控制电路内部计算机使用低电压(5~12V)和小电流(几毫安)，机床的外部电路则需要高电压(24、110 或 220V)和大电流(以安计量)，接口不仅要进行电压转换，而且必须对车间中经常存在的电流干扰加以过滤。这样的接口必须是用户针对不同应用来订做的。

PLC 可代替继电器设备工作。它们使用属于标准接线图的梯形图进行编程。与通用计算机一样，PLC 由 5 个主要部分组成：CPU(处理器)、内存、输入/输出(I/O)、电源、外围设备(如图 6.9 所示)。小型 PLC 如图 6.10 所示，它存在 16 个输入/输出点和一个标准的 RS-232 串行通信端口。

随着 PLC 的功能越来越灵活，高级语言也可以像低级语言那样用于编写程序。PLC 具有计算机的灵活性和标准简单的接口，便于连接程序和其他设备。从单个设备到非常复杂的制造工具，从简单的过程控制到制造系统监控，PLC被广泛应用于工业控制中。它们(PLC)可用于高速数据处理、高速数据通信、高级计算机语言支持中，当然也可用于基本过程控制中(如图6.11所示)。

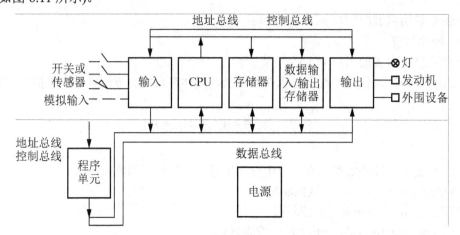

图6.9 可编程的控制器结构图

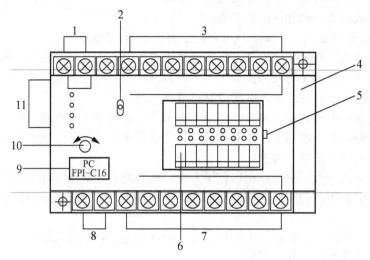

图6.10 FP1 C16控制面板

1—交流/直流电输入；2—模态选择；3—输出；4—输入/输出扩展槽；5—输入/输出状态灯；6—标签；7—输入；8—直流电输出；9—编程界面；10—可调节输入；11—PLC状态灯

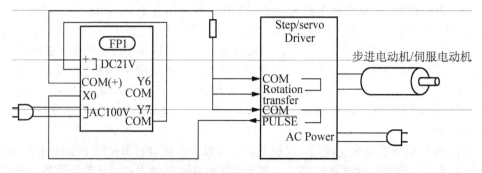

图6.11 PLC的应用(步进电动机/伺服电动机的控制)

制作继电器盘电路的模拟样板是一个单调的工作，需要精心计划和做大量工作，且调试和转换电路更为困难。可编程逻辑控制器通过软件编程取代了大量的线路，因此此项工作变得十分简单。由于线路、运动的机械零件和继电器触头大部分被软件所代替，因此(PLC)系统更加可靠。

6.8 特种加工方法

特种加工方法是一组采用多种技术去除多余材料的加工方法，这种方法将用到机械能、热能、电能、化学能或这些能量的组合，而不会用到在传统加工工艺中所用的锋利切削刀具。

特种加工方法又被称为先进的加工方法，当传统的诸如车、钻、铣及成型等加工方法由于以下一些特殊原因不适用或不够经济时，就需要用到特种加工方法。

(1) 硬度高且易脆的材料用传统加工方法很难用夹具夹紧。
(2) 工件很薄或易变性。
(3) 制件外形非常复杂。

1. 电火花加工

电火花加工(EDM)运用热电的方法，通过在工件和电极间产生大量不连续的电火花侵蚀工件上多余的材料。因此对于电火花加工来说，材料的硬度已不再重要。电火花加工示意图如图 6.12 所示，其中刀具和工件都属于绝缘体。电火花加工适用于成型硬度高、难以用车床加工的材料。用于锻造、冲压刀具、挤出模、航空和医疗方面的一些外形复杂、精确且不规则的零件都可以用电火花加工出来。用电火花加工出来的一些外形如图 6.13 所示。

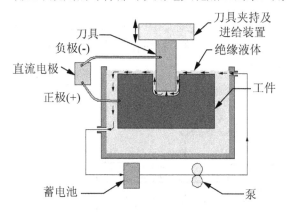

图 6.12 电火花加工示意图　　图 6.13 利用电火花加工的内部结构复杂的制件

电火花加工利用存储在电容器内的电流，使电流通过刀具阴极和工件阳极间的极小间隙来切除材料，该电流一般为 50V/10A。这样的高压导致在绝缘液体中出现了电场，这个电场存在于电极和工件间的细小间隙中，这导致悬浮于绝缘体中的导电粒子集中在电场强度最大的几个点。当电极与工件之间的电压差足够高时，绝缘液体突变，瞬间放出电火花穿过整个绝缘体，移除工件表面的部分材料。

应用于电火花加工的绝缘液体有烃油、煤油和脱离子剂。它的作用是充当刀具和工件之间的绝缘体、冷冻剂和冲洗金属屑的媒介。电火花加工中的电极一般由石墨、黄铜、红铜和铜-钨合金组成。

2. 线切割加工

电火花加工一般用于加工模具的机床和线切割机床 Wire EDM，如图 6.14 所示。在线切割加工中，金属丝沿设定路径缓慢移动，将工件上多余的材料去除。线切割加工利用电-热机械装置去除电传导材料。材料被存在于金属丝电极和工件间的绝缘液体所放出的大量离散电流所切除，当间隙内的液体被电离后，这些绝缘液体为每一次的放电创造了路径。发生放电的区域被加热到非常高的温度，因此制件表面被融化和切除。最终切除的金属屑被流动的绝缘液体冲洗掉。

利用线切割方法能为电子和航空航天工业切割复杂的零件，为模具制造业成型钢质工具，能以很高的精度切割圆柱形零件。

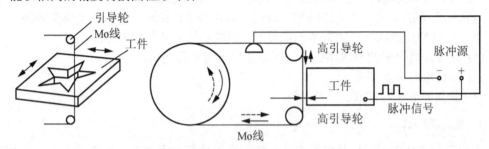

图 6.14 线切割加工示意图

线切割加工中的金属丝需要有较高的抗张强度和较好的电导率，一般由黄铜、红铜、钨、钼组成，锌或者镀铜金属丝也被广泛使用。

3. 电气化学加工

电气化学加工(ECM)是基于方向电镀原则的金属切削过程(如图 6.15 所示)。材料屑由工件阳极移向机床刀具阴极。电解液的流动可以使被侵蚀掉的材料在到达机床刀具(电极)之前被冲刷走。成型型腔内表面与刀具外形相一致。

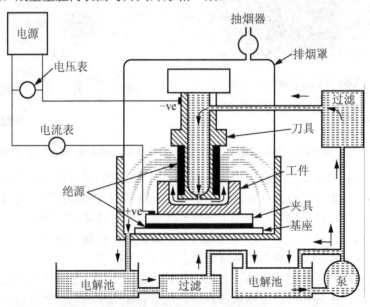

图 6.15 电气化学加工示意图

电气化学加工可用于电气化学修边、电弧加工、磨削、螺纹钻孔、精切修整等。

4. 超声加工

超声加工 USM，如图 6.16 所示是一种机械去除材料的方法，或称其为一种研磨方法，利用成型刀具、高频机械运动和研磨泥在又硬又脆的工件上侵蚀出孔洞或型腔。超声加工法可加工如单晶体、玻璃、多晶陶瓷等脆性材料和通过越来越复杂的操作来产生复杂外形和工件轮廓。研磨泥中的硬粒子在频率达到 100kHz 的震荡刀具的作用下加速移向工件表面。在重复的磨损下，刀具加工出横截面与其一致的型腔。

超声加工是一种在微观结构上不发生变化的非热能、非化学加工方法，工件和刀具的物理化学性质对于加工表面实质上没有任何影响。

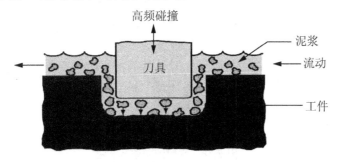

图 6.16　超声加工示意图

5. 激光加工

激光加工 LBM，如图 6.17 所示是一种利用热量去除材料的方法，它使用高能量的连续光束熔化金属或非金属工件表面的粒子，并使这些粒子汽化。激光可以用来切削、钻孔、焊接和作标记，激光加工特别适合用来加工精确定位孔。

可用于加工操作的激光类型有以下几种。

(1) CO_2(脉冲波或连续波)：一种气体激光器，可在红外线范围内发出光，可提供 25kW 的连续波。

(2) Nd-YAG(钇铝石榴石)：钇铝石榴石($Y_3Al_5O_{12}$)激光是一种使用电晶体的激光，可以在纤维光学电缆中传递光，可提供 50kW 的脉冲波和 1kW 的连续波。

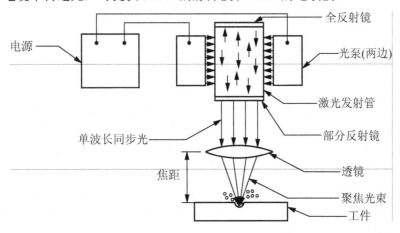

图 6.17　激光加工示意图

采用激光加工方法在难熔金属陶瓷和复合材料上不用弄弯工件就可以加工出直径为 0.005mm 的非常精确的孔洞。这种成型方法被广泛应用于金属或非金属材料上的钻孔和切削，激光加工将在电子和汽车工业方面获得更为广泛的应用。

6. 水射流切割

水射流切割(如图 6.18 所示)技术利用对水流加压，使得水流通过一个非常小的称为"口"或"钻石瓦"的出口。水射流切割利用水柱冲出出口去切割易切削材料，这种方法不适用于切割硬质材料。入口处的水流一般被加压到 1300~1400 巴，这样的高压水流被迫通过直径为 0.18～0.4mm 的细小出口。

图 6.18 水射流切割示意图

水射流切割可节省开支并通过排除或减少昂贵的次要加工来加速成型过程。由于材料不需要加热，切割刀口处只有细小的毛刺。这种成型方法减少了刀口破裂缺陷、结晶化、硬化、可焊接性能和机械加工性能降低等问题。

水射流切割主要用于切割低强度材料，如木材、塑料和铝。若加入了研磨剂(磨料水射流切割，如图 6.19 所示)，就可以切割如钢和工具钢这样的硬质材料。

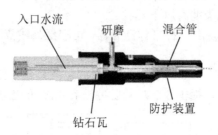

图 6.19 磨料水射流切割

7. 磨料水射流切割

磨料水射流切割是由水射流切割衍生而来的，在水射流加入了磨料微粒，如金刚砂、氧化铝等，提高了材料的切割率。无论何种类型的材料，从又硬又脆的材料如陶瓷、金属盒玻璃，到极软的材料如海绵和乳胶，基本上都可以用磨料水射流切割。细小的切割水流和由计算机控制的运动使得该方法可生产出高效精确的制件。这种加工方法尤其适用于那些无法用激光加工和热量切割的材料。不同厚度的金属、非金属和先进的复合材料都可以采用此方法切割。有些方法一边加工一边产生热量，因此不适合作用于热敏感材料，但磨料水射流切割可避免这样的问题。

磨料水射流切割被广泛应用于航空航天、汽车和电子工业中。航空航天工业中，军用飞机上的钛机身、机身组件(铝合金、钛合金、耐热合金)、铝制机身零件和内部机舱零件都是用磨料水射流切割法制造的。在汽车工业中，内部装饰(端部护顶梁、主体护顶梁、门板)和玻璃纤维车身组件和缓冲器也可用此法切割。同样地在电子工业中，电路板和电缆抽锭也可用此法切割。

项目7　模具的寿命与失效

7.1　模具的寿命与失效

选择的材料及模具加工方法是否合适在很大程度上决定了成型模具的使用寿命。更换模具有很多原因，例如由于磨损或塑性变形造成尺寸变化，成型表面腐蚀退化，润滑油作用损坏，以及开裂和细纹损坏。在热锻模具中模具失效的主要原因是侵蚀、热疲劳、机械疲劳和永久的塑性变形。

腐蚀，通常称为模具磨损，由于变形金属的压力及滑动导致的模具表面材料损失、模具材料磨损、模具表面温度、金属与模具接触表面相对滑动速度及接触层的特性是影响模具磨损的重要因素。

热疲劳在热锻压模具表面产生，可能导致热裂的产生。热疲劳的产生是由于模具表面与热变形金属的接触导致模具表面循环屈服所致。接触导致模具表面层扩大，由于温度梯度较高，表面层受到压应力作用。在足够高的温度下，这些压应力将导致表面层变形。当模具表面冷却时，产生相反的应力，表面层就处在拉伸状态。这种方式不断循环后，疲劳将导致裂纹出现，即所谓的热裂。

模具的开裂和细纹损坏是由于机械疲劳造成的，这种开裂和细纹损坏发生在模具过载和局部应力过高的情况下。由于加载或卸载使模具在变形过程中承受交变应力，而导致破裂产生，甚至导致模具失效。

模具的使用寿命和模具的失效在极大程度上要受到模具材料在已给定的成型加工工艺条件下所表现出的力学性能的影响。一般来说，这些性能与过程中的温度紧密相关，因此，冷成型模具材料与热成型模具材料非常不同。

当应用金属成型工艺连续生产不同种类的零件时，模具的设计加工及材料的选择就显得尤为重要。为了在可行的成本条件下提供可接受的模具寿命，必须采用合适的材料通过现代加工方法加工模具。通常一个成型过程的经济成功取决于模具寿命和每件模具的生产成本。对于给定的应用，适当的模具材料的选择取决于以下3个类型的变量。

(1) 与工艺本身相关的变量，包括模具型腔的尺寸、所采用的机床型号、变形速度、毛坯的初始尺寸、加工时的温度、润滑条件、生产率和零件批量。

(2) 模具载荷相关变量，包括加载速度即冲击或模具与变形金属间的接触时间(在热成型中接触时间尤为重要)、模具承受的最大载荷及压力、最大及最低模具温度、模具将承受的载荷循环数目。

(3) 模具材料的机械性能，包括淬透性、冲击强度、热强度(如果考虑热成型)、抗热性及机械疲劳。

7.2 模具中的表面处理及润滑

金属成形过程中常常伴随有热量的产生。塑性变形产生的热量和接口间的摩擦导致了一个既复杂又不断变化的温度场产生。由于温度分布会影响摩擦情况、变形金属的流动情况、零件精度及模具寿命，因此对成型过程温度场的预测就显得尤为重要。

模具的寿命取决于磨损、热裂、疲劳及塑性变形等因素。人们针对这些因素对模具寿命的影响已做了很多研究。一般来说，当模具在重复操作中，包括热软化锻压过程，温度不断升高时，模具的表面硬度降低。热软化加速模具表面的磨损、热裂、疲劳及塑性变形。

为了加长模具的使用寿命，必须通过热处理来增加模具的表面硬度，同时也需要对表面进行处理来减小摩擦及增加热绝缘性。通过表面处理可有效改变模具的热学性能。

润滑的作用在于减少在成型加工过程中模具和工件间产生的摩擦以及从钢坯向模具进行对的热传递。石墨，一种固体润滑剂，在热锻压之前被喷在模具或坯料上。不同的石墨使得坯料与模具间的热传导系数不同。另外，选择合适的润滑剂可以减小坯料与模具间的热传导系数，延长模具寿命。

影响模具使用寿命的主要因素是与热软化作用相关的表面热处理和润滑。高表面硬度和低热传导系数可增长模具的有效使用寿命。

References

[1] Betzalel Avitzur. Handbook of Metal-forming Processes[M]. New York: John Wiley & Sons Inc., 1983.

[2] Klaus Stoeckhert. Mold-making Handbook for the Plastics Engineer[M]. New York: Hanser Publishers, 1983.

[3] John R. Lindbeck. Manufacturing Technology[M]. New Jersey: Prentice Hau, 1990.

[4] E. Paul De Garmo, JT. Black, Ronald A. Kohser. Materials and Processes in Manufacturing[M]. London: Macmillan Publishing Company, 1997.

[5] Paul Kennenth Wright. 21st Century Manufacturing[M]. 北京：清华大学出版社，2002.

[6] Peter Smid. CNC Machining and Programming[M]. Second Edition. New York: U.S.A Industrial Inc., 2003.

[7] Eric H. Glendinning. Oxford English for Electrical and Mechanical Engineering[M]. Oxford: Oxford University Press, 1995.

[8] Serope Kalpakjian, Steven R. Sschmid. Manufacturing Engineering and Technology[M]. 5th ed..New Jersey: Prentice Hall, 2006.

[9] R. L. Timings, S. P. Wilkinson. Manufacturing Technology (Volume 2)[M]. Hong Kong: Longman, 2000.

[10] E. Paul DeGarmo, J.T. Black, R.A. Kohsern. Materials and Processes in Manufacturing. 8th ed.. New Jersey: Prentice-Hall, 1997: 941~947.

[11] 清华大学. 英汉技术词典[M]. 北京：国防工业出版社，1978.

[12] 阎庆甲，阎文培. 科技英语翻译方法[M]. 北京：冶金工业出版社，1992.

[13] 上海职教课程改革和教材建设委员会. 机电与数控专业英语[M]. 北京：机械工业出版社，2001.

[14] 王晓江. 模具设计与制造专业英语[M]. 北京：机械工业出版社，2001.

[15] 胡礼木，王卫卫. 材料成形及控制工程专业英语阅读[M]. 北京：机械工业出版社，2004.

[16] 夏琴香. 冲压成形工艺及模具设计[M]. 广州：华南理工大学出版社，2004.

[17] 张晓黎. 塑料加工和模具专业英语[M]. 北京：化学工业出版社，2005.

[18] 董建国. 机械专业英语[M]. 西安：西安电子科技大学出版社，2005.

[19] 章跃. 机械制造专业英语[M]. 北京：机械工业出版社，2006.

[20] 杨成美. 模具专业英语[M]. 大连：大连理工大学出版社，2007.

北京大学出版社高职高专机电系列规划教材

序号	书号	书名	编著者	定价	出版日期
1	978-7-301-12181-8	自动控制原理与应用	梁南丁	23.00	2012.1 第3次印刷
2	978-7-5038-4869-8	设备状态监测与故障诊断技术	林英志	22.00	2013.2 第4次印刷
3	978-7-301-13262-3	实用数控编程与操作	钱东东	32.00	2011.8 第3次印刷
4	978-7-301-13383-5	机械专业英语图解教程	朱派龙	22.00	2013.1 第5次印刷
5	978-7-301-13582-2	液压与气压传动技术	袁 广	24.00	2011.3 第3次印刷
6	978-7-301-13662-1	机械制造技术	宁广庆	42.00	2010.11 第2次印刷
7	978-7-301-13574-7	机械制造基础	徐从清	32.00	2012.7 第3次印刷
8	978-7-301-13653-9	工程力学	武昭晖	25.00	2011.2 第3次印刷
9	978-7-301-13652-2	金工实训	柴增田	22.00	2013.1 第4次印刷
10	978-7-301-14470-1	数控编程与操作	刘瑞已	29.00	2011.2 第2次印刷
11	978-7-301-13651-5	金属工艺学	柴增田	27.00	2011.6 第2次印刷
12	978-7-301-12389-8	电机与拖动	梁南丁	32.00	2011.12 第2次印刷
13	978-7-301-13659-1	CAD/CAM实体造型教程与实训(Pro/ENGINEER版)	诸小丽	38.00	2012.1 第3次印刷
14	978-7-301-13656-0	机械设计基础	时忠明	25.00	2012.7 第3次印刷
15	978-7-301-17122-6	AutoCAD机械绘图项目教程	张海鹏	36.00	2011.10 第2次印刷
16	978-7-301-17148-6	普通机床零件加工	杨雪青	26.00	2010.6
17	978-7-301-17398-5	数控加工技术项目教程	李东君	48.00	2010.8
18	978-7-301-17573-6	AutoCAD机械绘图基础教程	王长忠	32.00	2010.8
19	978-7-301-17557-6	CAD/CAM数控编程项目教程(UG版)	慕 灿	45.00	2012.4 第2次印刷
20	978-7-301-17609-2	液压传动	龚肖新	22.00	2010.8
21	978-7-301-17679-5	机械零件数控加工	李 文	38.00	2010.8
22	978-7-301-17608-5	机械加工工艺编制	于爱武	45.00	2012.2 第2次印刷
23	978-7-301-17707-5	零件加工信息分析	谢 蕾	46.00	2010.8
24	978-7-301-18357-1	机械制图	徐连孝	27.00	2012.9 第2次印刷
25	978-7-301-18143-0	机械制图习题集	徐连孝	20.00	2011.1
26	978-7-301-18470-7	传感器检测技术及应用	王晓敏	35.00	2012.7 第2次印刷
27	978-7-301-18471-4	冲压工艺与模具设计	张 芳	39.00	2011.3
28	978-7-301-18852-1	机电专业英语	戴正阳	28.00	2011.5
29	978-7-301-19272-6	电气控制与PLC程序设计(松下系列)	姜秀玲	36.00	2011.8
30	978-7-301-19297-9	机械制造工艺及夹具设计	徐 勇	28.00	2011.8
31	978-7-301-19319-8	电力系统自动装置	王 伟	24.00	2011.8
32	978-7-301-19374-7	公差配合与技术测量	庄佃霞	26.00	2011.8
33	978-7-301-19436-2	公差与测量技术	余 键	25.00	2011.9
34	978-7-301-19010-4	AutoCAD机械绘图基础教程与实训(第2版)	欧阳全会	36.00	2013.1 第2次印刷
35	978-7-301-19638-0	电气控制与PLC应用技术	郭 燕	24.00	2012.1
36	978-7-301-19933-6	冷冲压工艺与模具设计	刘洪贤	32.00	2012.1
37	978-7-301-20002-5	数控机床故障诊断与维修	陈学军	38.00	2012.1
38	978-7-301-20312-5	数控编程与加工项目教程	周晓宏	42.00	2012.3
39	978-7-301-20414-6	Pro/ENGINEER Wildfire产品设计项目教程	罗 岩	31.00	2012.5
40	978-7-301-15692-6	机械制图	吴百中	26.00	2012.7 第2次印刷
41	978-7-301-20945-5	数控铣削技术	陈晓罗	42.00	2012.7
42	978-7-301-21053-6	数控车削技术	王军红	28.00	2012.8
43	978-7-301-21119-9	数控机床及其维护	黄应勇	38.00	2012.8
44	978-7-301-20752-9	液压传动与气动技术(第2版)	曹建东	40.00	2012.8
45	978-7-301-18630-5	电机与电力拖动	孙英伟	33.00	2011.3
46	978-7-301-16448-8	Pro/ENGINEER Wildfire 设计实训教程	吴志清	38.00	2012.8
47	978-7-301-21239-4	自动生产线安装与调试实训教程	周 洋	30.00	2012.9
48	978-7-301-21269-1	电机控制与实践	徐 锋	34.00	2012.9
49	978-7-301-16770-0	电机拖动与应用实训教程	任娟平	36.00	2012.11
50	978-7-301-20654-6	自动生产线调试与维护	吴有明	28.00	2013.1
51	978-7-301-21988-1	普通机床的检修与维护	宋亚林	33.00	2013.1
52	978-7-301-21873-0	CAD/CAM数控编程项目教程(CAXA版)	刘玉春	42.00	2013.3
53	978-7-301-22315-4	低压电气控制安装与调试实训教程	张 郭	24.00	2013.4
54	978-7-301-19848-3	机械制造综合设计及实训	裴俊彦	37.00	2013.4
55	978-7-301-22632-2	机床电气控制与维修	崔兴艳	28.00	2013.7
56	978-7-301-22672-8	机电设备控制基础	王本铁	32.00	2013.7
57	978-7-301-22678-0	模具专业英语图解教程	李东君	22.00	2013.7

北京大学出版社高职高专电子信息系列规划教材

序号	书号	书名	编著者	定价	出版日期
1	978-7-301-12180-1	单片机开发应用技术	李国兴	21.00	2010.9 第 2 次印刷
2	978-7-301-12386-7	高频电子线路	李福勤	20.00	2013.2 第 3 次印刷
3	978-7-301-12384-3	电路分析基础	徐 锋	22.00	2010.3 第 2 次印刷
4	978-7-301-13572-3	模拟电子技术及应用	刁修睦	28.00	2012.8 第 3 次印刷
5	978-7-301-12390-4	电力电子技术	梁南丁	29.00	2010.7 第 2 次印刷
6	978-7-301-12383-6	电气控制与PLC(西门子系列)	李 伟	26.00	2012.3 第 2 次印刷
7	978-7-301-12387-4	电子线路CAD	殷庆纵	28.00	2012.7 第 4 次印刷
8	978-7-301-12382-9	电气控制及PLC应用(三菱系列)	华满香	24.00	2012.5 第 2 次印刷
9	978-7-301-16898-1	单片机设计应用与仿真	陆旭明	26.00	2012.4 第 2 次印刷
10	978-7-301-16830-1	维修电工技能与实训	陈学平	37.00	2010.7
11	978-7-301-17324-4	电机控制与应用	魏润仙	34.00	2010.8
12	978-7-301-17569-9	电工电子技术项目教程	杨德明	32.00	2012.4 第 2 次印刷
13	978-7-301-17696-2	模拟电子技术	蒋 然	35.00	2010.8
14	978-7-301-17712-9	电子技术应用项目式教程	王志伟	32.00	2012.7 第 2 次印刷
15	978-7-301-17730-3	电力电子技术	崔 红	23.00	2010.9
16	978-7-301-17877-5	电子信息专业英语	高金玉	26.00	2011.11 第 2 次印刷
17	978-7-301-17958-1	单片机开发入门及应用实例	熊华波	30.00	2011.1
18	978-7-301-18188-1	可编程控制器应用技术项目教程(西门子)	崔维群	38.00	2013.6 第 2 次印刷
19	978-7-301-18322-9	电子EDA技术(Multisim)	刘训非	30.00	2012.7 第 2 次印刷
20	978-7-301-18144-7	数字电子技术项目教程	冯泽虎	28.00	2011.1
21	978-7-301-18519-3	电工技术应用	孙建领	26.00	2011.3
22	978-7-301-18770-8	电机应用技术	郭宝宁	33.00	2011.5
23	978-7-301-18520-9	电子线路分析与应用	梁玉国	34.00	2011.7
24	978-7-301-18622-0	PLC与变频器控制系统设计与调试	姜永华	34.00	2011.6
25	978-7-301-19310-5	PCB板的设计与制作	夏淑丽	33.00	2011.8
26	978-7-301-19326-6	综合电子设计与实践	钱卫钧	25.00	2011.8
27	978-7-301-19302-0	基于汇编语言的单片机仿真教程与实训	张秀国	32.00	2011.8
28	978-7-301-19153-8	数字电子技术与应用	宋雪臣	33.00	2011.9
29	978-7-301-19525-3	电工电子技术	倪 涛	38.00	2011.9
30	978-7-301-19953-4	电子技术项目教程	徐超明	38.00	2012.1
31	978-7-301-20000-1	单片机应用技术教程	罗国荣	40.00	2012.2
32	978-7-301-20009-4	数字逻辑与微机原理	宋振辉	49.00	2012.1
33	978-7-301-20706-2	高频电子技术	朱小样	32.00	2012.6
34	978-7-301-21055-0	单片机应用项目化教程	顾亚文	32.00	2012.8
35	978-7-301-17489-0	单片机原理及应用	陈高锋	32.00	2012.9
36	978-7-301-21147-2	Protel 99 SE 印制电路板设计案例教程	王 静	35.00	2012.8
37	978-7-301-19639-7	电路分析基础(第2版)	张丽萍	25.00	2012.9
38	978-7-301-22362-8	电子产品组装与调试实训教程	何 杰	28.00	2013.6
39	978-7-301-22546-2	电工技能实训教程	韩亚军	22.00	2013.6
40	978-7-301-22390-1	单片机开发与实践教程	宋玲玲	24.00	2013.6

相关教学资源如电子课件、电子教材、习题答案等可以登录 www.pup6.com 下载或在线阅读。

扑六知识网(www.pup6.com)有海量的相关教学资源和电子教材供阅读及下载(包括北京大学出版社第六事业部的相关资源),同时欢迎您将教学课件、视频、教案、素材、习题、试卷、辅导材料、课改成果、设计作品、论文等教学资源上传到 pup6.com,与全国高校师生分享您的教学成就与经验,并可自由设定价格,知识也能创造财富。具体情况请登录网站查询。

如您需要免费纸质样书用于教学,欢迎登录第六事业部门户网(www.pup6.cn)填表申请,并欢迎在线登记选题以到北京大学出版社来出版您的大作,也可下载相关表格填写后发到我们的邮箱,我们将及时与您取得联系并做好全方位的服务。

扑六知识网将打造成全国最大的教育资源共享平台,欢迎您的加入——让知识有价值,让教学无界限,让学习更轻松。

联系方式:010-62750667、yongjian3000@163.com、linzhangbo@126.com,欢迎来电来信。